Greetings from Canada

Greetings from Canada

Postcards from Dutch Immigrants to the Netherlands

1884–1915

JAN KRIJFF

KAREN GREEN

GRANVILLE ISLAND
PUBLISHING

Library and Archives Canada Cataloguing in Publication

Krijff, Jan Th. J., 1947–
    Greetings from Canada : postcards from Dutch immigrants to the Netherlands, 1884-1915 / Jan Krijff, Karen Green.

 Includes bibliographical references and index.
ISBN 978-1-926991-17-7

    1. Dutch—Canada—Correspondence. 2. Immigrants—Canada—Correspondence. 3. Dutch—Canada—History. 4. Netherlands—Emigration and immigration—History. 5. Canada—Emigration and immigration—History. 6. Postcards—Canada—History. I. Green, Karen, 1956– II. Title.

FC106.D9K75 2012   971'.0043931   C2012-907814-X

Editor: Kyle Hawke
Indexer: Renée Fossett
Cover and Text Designer: Omar Gallegos

Granville Island Publishing Ltd.
212 – 1656 Duranleau St. Granville Island
Vancouver, BC, Canada V6H 3S4

604-688-0320 / 1-877-688-0320
info@granvilleislandpublishing.com
www.granvilleislandpublishing.com

First Published in 2013
Second Printing in 2015
Printed in Canada on recycled paper

To our Aunt Ine*

Spurred on by her father to obtain an excellent education, Ine graduated from
Utrechts Stedelijk Gymnasium. This venerable institution reinforced her life-long
love of the arts and literature, which she generously fostered in others.

*(Marchina Anna Krijff, Alkmaar 1913 – Eindhoven 2011)

Table of Contents

About the Cover Image

The cover photograph, circa 1908, shows two Dutch fellows, F. Hassink and Gerhardus Warnerus ten Bruggencate (on the right holding a gun) standing near a tent, likely pitched in the region of Prince Albert, Saskatchewan.

They could not have known their fates; nor could anyone guess merely by looking at this picture. Their respective lives are now part of history. Just days before publishing this book, with one more attempt to find additional information about these two men — there it was — ten Bruggencate was murdered in February of 1913 by two Hungarian immigrants.

Turning a page in an old register, surfing the web, talking to a family member, engaging staff in libraries, scrolling through film and fiche in an archive — all may send you to a past you never imagined. Discovery and story, the very stuff of historical and genealogical research.

Foreword

Some forty years have passed since I first began my study of Dutch immigration to Canada. In the course of that work I have been fortunate to have had access to both Dutch and Canadian government records, the archives of Dutch emigration societies and the remembrances of immigrants who have had the opportunity to record their experiences in some manner or other. It soon became clear to me that the first generation immigrants seldom kept diaries, wrote books or carried on extended correspondence. Many were limited by their lack of education and the necessity to carve out a living in their new Homeland. For the researcher, the most viable remaining source of information was personal interviews with the immigrants, but they were limited by the aging of the population. As time passes, the researcher is forced to look for alternative ways to recapture the immigrant experience.

Jan Krijff, although, or because, he is not an academic historian, has been drawn to those alternative sources that others have ignored. As a true "amateur" historian, he joins the great number of people who do history for the love of it, and in so doing opens up new and interesting perspectives on Dutch immigration to Canada. Combining his hobby of postcard collecting with his knowledge of Dutch society at the turn of the nineteenth century and the forces that drove emigration, Krijff has been able to construct a clearer picture of the role that class played in the movement. Rich adventurers joined those who were looking for the "Land of the Second Chance". The humble postcard, the "Twitter" of its age, reveals the hopes of the poor and the assumptions of the well-to-do in a few well-chosen words. Some promise a letter to come, others leave a message that may be the last the people at home will hear from the aspirant immigrant. Only time will tell and the postcard must suffice.

Jan Krijff, because of his unique experiences, is probably the only one who could have assembled *Greetings from Canada* from his collection of postcards and given them a new form that helps explain the beginnings of Dutch immigration to Canada. He has combined the postcards with relevant pictures, documents and other ephemera that expand the relevance of the postcard and make it an important new historical resource in the jigsaw puzzle of history.

Herman Ganzevoort
Professor Emeritus
University of Calgary
November 12, 2012

Preface

Dear Cousin.

I still receive your papers, many thanks for that. John and I have each taken up 160 acres of land. I think next week I will start building a house and start plowing my property. John is presently teaching again; he makes f 75.00 a month. At the moment we have nice weather. Greetings to you and to your fiancée also from John.

From your affectionate cousin, P. Goossen

Pilot-Mound, July 1888
address now P. Goossen Bristol-City, Mant-N. Am

Two brothers, Pieter and Johannes Goossen, from a well-to-do family in Vlissingen, emigrated to Canada in 1887. Their father Willem Goossen was a medical doctor. They first settled on two quarter-sections (NW 1/4, SW 1/4 S-6, T-3, R-12, W of 1st) near Pilot Mound, Manitoba, and later farmed three quarters near Enderby, British Columbia. Pieter Goossen died August 24, 1932, in Vancouver.

A Remarkable Find

These few words penned in 1888 onto this small card are from Pieter Goossen to his cousin Johannes Gideon Siegers, a banker in Amsterdam. They provide very personal insight into Pieter's new life in Canada. Personal testimonies by immigrants of more than one hundred years ago are scarce. They are seldom found in official records and statistics, which are often the main source of information about the broader immigrant experience. Such 'ego-documents'[1] are historically and socially valuable. This card, in Goossen's own hand, has survived the times — by holding it and reading it, you can be in touch with the writer. Moreover, you are, perhaps, prompted to ponder more deeply about these times gone by.

I came across this card in an antique shop in Calgary, in the early 1970s. The proprietor was Sam C. Nickle, a prominent citizen and acclaimed stamp collector. Knowing my country of birth, he urged me to buy this scarce item. He even made me a special offer! Quite frankly, it was a great surprise to stumble upon this card. After a quick read, I became acutely aware of its relevance to the history of Dutch immigration to Canada. Furthermore, this serendipitous experience was the first time I became aware of early Dutch immigration to Canada. In Holland, little is known about emigration to Canada before 1915, contrasting with the widely known emigration wave to Canada that took place right after the Second World War.

Having carefully stored this one-off purchase of ephemera for many years, it was not until I had started my research about Dutch emigration to Winnipeg that I began to collect Canadian postcards mailed before 1915 by Dutch immigrants to The Netherlands. It turned out that finding picture postcards with personal notes, also known as 'mini-diaries'[2], was mostly dependent upon sheer luck.

In her work about ego-documents, published in the *Encyclopedia of European Social History*, Mary Lindemann refers to the importance of these mini-diaries as "endowing ordinary lives with agency, dignity, and texture".[3] This comment, inspired me to share this collection, of about 175 cards, with a wider public. With this book, I also wish to preserve and to bring to light previously untold stories from people of various backgrounds who left The Netherlands on an adventure to Canada in search of a better life. By this action, the immigrants and their stories became part of Canada's rich history.

Jan Krijff

Introduction

Why Picture Postcards?

"Postcards form a constitutive part of the way in which the business of art, commerce, history, and identity is negotiated on a daily basis" (*Postcards: Ephemeral Histories of Modernity*).[4]

For most of us it is difficult to abruptly break with our direct past, our homes and our neighbourhoods, our families and our friends. To make the shift to a new country a little easier, many Dutch emigrants, when possible, chose to settle in towns and villages in Canada where a Dutch connection already existed. There, they could get support and were also able to share their common past, language, and culture, which probably eased their transition to Canadian life.

A few may well have emigrated in order to break with the past; but the large majority of emigrants, who had made the move with a better future in mind, still maintained the desire to preserve their roots. Therefore, the move to a new country did create dislocation from 'home'. One way to deal with this and find solace was by writing home in order to keep in contact with family and friends.

Currently, there are many ways to keep in touch with loved ones in the old country: by texting, Skyping and emailing from our homes or any other place in the world. At the turn of the 20th century, however, life was simpler, and emigrants relied on the humble letter or postcard. In particular, picture postcards, which cost less to send, were used extensively during the 'Golden Age of Postcards' referring to the period between 1900 and the beginning of World War I in 1914.

The postcard, the precursor of the 'picture postcard', originated in Austria where the first official postal stationary card (with a pre-printed government stamp) was sent on October 1, 1869. Other countries would soon follow suit. In Canada, the first official postcard was issued on June 1, 1872, being the first outside of Europe. The private postcard was available after January 1, 1895, but regulations did not allow images. The stamp and address had to be placed on one side and the written message on the other side. Within a short period the regulations were relaxed but it was not until 1903 that Canada permitted the so-called 'postcard with divided back', which is still in use today.

To decorate the message cards with photographic images required new technology including mass printing and mass production. By then, progress in new copy techniques and procedures had reached a point that cheap picture postcards were manufactured in large enough quantities to have become part of our culture. In Canada at that time, well-known publishers of picture postcards were: Illustrated Postcard Co. (Montreal,1902), Montreal Import Co. (c. 1901), Valentine & Sons (1903) and W.G. MacFarlane (1905), both in Toronto. Postcards depicting small towns and villages were not usually issued by the large publishing companies. Most of the examples depicting small-town views (which are generally difficult to find) were made by local photographers and often sold by local storekeepers.

By the early 1900s, picture postcards were not used only for correspondence. They also became collectable, a phenomenon exploited by manufacturers through issuing cards in 'series' and in 'theme' formats. Collecting became a frenzy that also crossed borders. The commercial world seized advantage by developing and selling a wide variety of albums for collectors. Advertisements for postcard pen pals were placed in special postcard club magazines, which were read around the world. Some cards bear membership numbers of postcard clubs. Many cards were mailed from many different countries having inscriptions such as "please exchange cards". Cards between Canada and The Netherlands were no exception.

The growing numbers of people on the move in the world in addition to the rapid increase in business communications gave rise to a modern and functional global postal system. This meant that the Canadian postal service kept pace, allowing the ordinary immigrant to maintain connections through sending picture postcards, which were less costly than sending letters.

There are no exact numbers of Dutch immigrants nor of the extent to which picture postcards were used during the period covered by this book. The same can be said about the numbers of cards that are still, perhaps, held somewhere. A number of examples are stored in libraries and archives. An unknown number are likely to be found in private collections. Perhaps many cards are still in the hands of families related to the writers. It is also not unreasonable to conclude that many of the cards no longer exist. Fire damage, water damage, the negative effects of neglect, or simply discarding them must have reduced the numbers of cards left, limiting the opportunities to find them.

Not all of the collection is in this book. To make the cut, a card must have written text on the back — even if it simply conveys greetings, a name, a birthday wish, concern about a health situation, or congratulations on the birth of child. The cards must be from an immigrant, not just a visitor, which is sometimes difficult to ascertain. In some cases there are multiple cards from one person. No matter the message, we gain some insight into the writers' thoughts, and sometimes how their daily life was influenced by the surroundings and culture of the new country.

Going behind the writing on the backs of the cards required translation and detective work. Translation is not without challenges. Some of the cards have beautifully clear handwriting while that of others is nearly impossible to decipher. Also, the quality of the grammar and spelling differs greatly, providing some indications as to the level of education obtained by the immigrant. In addition, some of the cards were from immigrants from Holland who wrote in German or French. This may mean that they or their parents had earlier immigrated to Holland before moving on to Canada. The western part of Holland was very much a destination for immigrants from other parts of Europe. There was sleuthing required to explain a bit about the writers and receivers. This meant being able to track down the addresses of the recipients, knowing more about them, and then working backwards to the sender, if clues were found. In some cases, the names had been deliberately obliterated.

Looking at the places where the cards originated, we see that the majority were mailed from the Prairie provinces. This clearly reflects the Canadian system of immigrant recruitment, which was predicated upon populating and developing the western provinces. On the other hand, the destinations for most of the cards were the larger cities in heavily populated areas of the western part of The Netherlands. This may be counter-intuitive. It is a commonly-held belief that most Dutch immigrants were from the less-developed northern and eastern parts of the country.

Not only do we discover some names of the towns and villages in Holland (even the colony of the Dutch East Indies) where the recipients lived, but we also find more about where the immigrants settled in Canada. Most of the picture postcards showing scenes of Canada convey an impression of places where the writers lived, or perhaps as examples of Canadian landscapes, so vastly different than where they came from. Many of these sites are still intact or little changed, while others have disappeared completely, making the postcard one part of the record of its existence.

Life continued in the new country, despite the differences in culture and surroundings. It remained important to recognize occasions such as the New Year, so we see a substantial number of these cards.

We also see many cards which simply serve as a reminder to the folks at home that they are not forgotten. These cards bear short messages such as "many greetings" and in several cases only a first name or initial and no written message, at all. Fortunately, a significant number of cards have much more to say, which increases the value of compiling them for publication.

The cards were collected essentially at random. Even so, it is possible to create a picture of the immigrant experience by weaving them together in common themes. The structure of the book, then, starts at the beginning with first landing in Canada, and follows life through to choices to stay or return home.

Dutch Immigration to Canada

"Thinking of Holland
I see broad rivers
Move slowly through
unending lowlands."
— Hendrik Marsman

Since the 16th century, the country of The Netherlands, nestled where the North Sea leans against the land, has depended largely on commerce and trade. Over time, it became an important independent seafaring nation, motivating a number of its enterprising inhabitants to swarm around the world in search of new business opportunities. In order to facilitate the growing trade of the 16th and 17th centuries, the Dutch government established diplomatic relations with many countries. This in turn allowed the Dutch to set up trading posts, sometimes in far-flung places, a number of which would develop into small, yet flourishing, Dutch settlements.

Holland's insatiable appetite for profit, at that time, was the driving force to become a major commercial contender on the world scene. It succeeded and remains a wealthy nation today. To achieve this objective, it had diversified its interests and scrambled for influence in the Atlantic zone. By 1609, with respect to the North American continent, this had resulted in the creation of a settlement called New Amsterdam, later to become New York City. Despite high expectations of what the new territory could offer, it did not generate the anticipated profits. By 1650, Dutch commercial interest in building a colony had waned and lost financial support from the government of The Netherlands. It was not long thereafter that the British took possession of New York.

These events did not, however, persuade the Dutch to avert their gaze from the USA. In spite of British rule, and on a decidedly smaller scale, family contacts and trade relations between Holland and New York did continue. Illustrative of this relationship is the activity amongst the higher-ranks, taking place during the time leading up to American Independence. The non-Loyalist Americans needed cash and appealed to the Amsterdam financial community for assistance.[5] With respect to immigration, for the Dutch the USA has been by far the most desired destination. Firstly, in the 1840's and 1850's, Dutch people immigrated mainly to Michigan and Iowa, for religious reasons. During the 1880's and 1890's, a period of economic malaise in Holland, a much larger wave followed, settling across the USA. To the present day, the Dutch have remained fascinated with all facets of the USA, still a close ally and important trading partner, as well as an attractive emigration destination.

In great contrast is the manner in which relations between the Netherlands and Canada developed. Firstly, there was no Dutch settlement in 17th century Canada which could have created connections between the two nations. Due to British laws in force[6] restricting shipping to Canada during the 17th, 18th, and early 19th centuries, no direct trade relations could be formally established between the two countries, preventing any awareness or potential for relationships to be established. It was not until 1862, some time after the trade restrictions were lifted, that Canada came into in the picture as a country meriting official relations. In that year, The Netherlands appointed Benjamin Homer-Dixon as the first Dutch consul to Canada, based in Toronto.[7]

With respect to Dutch immigration to Canada during the 17th century, there is no evidence of any substantial activity. However during that time, contacts were made between Dutch sailors and coastal inhabitants of Newfoundland and with Inuit people in Davis Strait.

During the 18th century, the city of Rotterdam was a main transit port for many European immigrants heading to North America. The city was an important place for Palatinate immigrants (mostly German and Swiss) on their journey to the USA. However, during 1751 and 1752, a small number of ships with Palatinates departed from Rotterdam bound for Halifax. These vessels were chartered by John Dick of Rotterdam whom the British Government had hired to procure Protestant immigrants for Nova Scotia. Three of his ships, *Pearl*, *Betty*, and *Speedwell* carried a small number of Dutch immigrants.[8] On *Speedwell*, which sailed in May of 1751, a few were from the province of Friesland and nine were from the province of Groningen. One of the Frisians was the watch-maker Thomas W. Itsinga, who emigrated with his family. He eventually became known as a silversmith in Halifax.[9]

Since that time, incidents of Dutch immigration were few and far-between. We know of some. Jasper van der Sluys came to Canada and worked for a short time between 1815–1820 as a bookkeeper for the North West Company in Montreal.[10] It was the front of an envelope shown in a auction catalogue that led me to Arie van der Hart from Hoogblokland, who arrived in 1871 in Canada and settled in Berlin (now Waterloo), Ontario where he set up his tailor shop.[11] On the west coast of Canada a few years later, in 1877, Rhynvis Offerhaus arrived in Victoria, BC, where he would earn his living by being a teacher. Five years later, Edo Offerhaus (a young physician of the same family) from Nieuwolda would land in Spallumcheen, British Columbia. In 1882, his wedding announcement appeared in a Dutch newspaper, *Het nieuws van den Dag*.[12] Up to then, Dutch emigration to Canada was insignificant and consequently left unattended by the Canadian government.

Things would change in 1883 when the laying of railway steel reached Calgary, an important moment in history, marking the start of European settlement in the Canadian West. Under the watchful eyes of Renee H. H. toe Laer, promotional campaigns were commenced across the entire European continent, aiming to entice emigrants to Canada's West. In May of 1883, the Dutch, in particular, had an opportunity to get a closer look at Canada. In trying to sell the 'Canadian Dream', with the promise of free land and unlimited opportunities, the CPR prepared an elaborate display, mostly of agricultural products, at the International Colonial and Export Exhibition in Amsterdam.[13] This initiative was developed in conjunction with a few Dutch bankers who were financially involved in the CPR, and who would prosper from emigrants settling in Canada. It is, of course, impossible to measure the effectiveness of the CPR's participation in the exhibition. However, the evidence suggests that after the big event, only a handful of Dutch people immigrated to Canada. It is possible that prospective immigrant settlers did not attend, or perhaps only the entries of the more exotic countries present were of interest to those who did attend. It does appear that the few we know of who journeyed to Canada following the exhibition were mostly members of the Dutch upper class.

While the early efforts of the CPR to persuade large numbers of ordinary Dutch people to immigrate to Canada did not yield the desired results, the concept of Canada as an emigration destination did appeal to some. One such gentleman, who greatly appreciated Canada's potential for immigrants, was Lodewijk R. J. A. Roosmale Nepveu, a high-ranking military officer and a member of the Dutch upper class. He recognized that the global economic crisis of 1892 had had dire consequences for working class people in The Netherlands. Being active in the Christian Revival Movement, Roosmale Nepveu was concerned about the exceptionally precarious situation of many impoverished citizens living in the province of Friesland and the instability that this could cause to the nation's political system. The best way to relieve the poor of their horrendous circumstances was to encourage them to emigrate to a Christian and civilized environment. In his view, this lifestyle was more possible in Canada than it would have been in the USA. His bias towards Canada was probably influenced by his son, Henri, who had already immigrated to Yorkton, N.W.T. (now Saskatchewan) in 1888.

To realize this aspiration, Roosmale Nepveu established a committee to promote and support Dutch people emigrating, aiding them by organizing transportation to western Canada. On February 15, 1892, the first meeting of the so-called Committee of Immigration was held in Utrecht. The work of the committee, which also included collecting enough money to finance its work, bore fruit. On April 1, 1893, a group of 68 Dutch emigrants boarded a vessel in the Amsterdam harbour, headed for Canada via Liverpool, England.[14]

On April 22, 1893, this group arrived safely after enduring the Atlantic crossing on the *Numidian*, followed by a few days' train ride toward the CPR station in Winnipeg. Upon arriving there, they were greeted by Robbert Insinger, another Dutch immigrant of considerable means, who would further assist them in setting up their lives in Canada's 'Wild West'.

Initially, living conditions in Canada for many of this group were extremely difficult and discouraging, mainly through lack of work and inadequate housing. It was not long afterward that many sought out better conditions. Records suggest that most of them ended up in Winnipeg, forming a small Dutch nucleus, huddling together, providing each other with some measure of protection and social support. Two such survivors, Klaas de Jong and Walle Heeres, put their stories of hardship and perseverance to paper.[15] Other brave members of their group who must have shared similar experiences have been hidden from our view, perhaps anonymously assimilating into Canada's mosaic.

In July 1897, a piece appeared in the *Algemeen Handelsblad* about the committee called the "Vereening tot bevordering van emigratie". It was willing to organize settlement in Canada for those who were able to pay their own way.[16] Interested parties were to apply to Johannes H. F. Gangel in Harderwijk. In addition, an appeal for money was made to help indigent people. It would appear that this campaign was not successful. This is not to say that Dutch people stopped emigrating to Canada. To the contrary, they did continue on an individual basis. However, due to imperfect records, there is no clear picture about the exact numbers and locations of where they settled.

Immigration had become easier after 1896 when the Canadian government initiated a more deliberate immigration policy in order to expand the country's economy. Under the determined leadership of Clifford Sifton, the Minister of the Interior, strategies were put into place to accelerate the population of the Prairies with immigrants. A network of recruitment agencies was put to work, particularly in order to attract farmers and farm labourers. However, it still would take a few years before the campaign was to be active in Holland. This was usually through newspaper advertisements or articles extolling the virtues of Canada. In 1903, a rather cautiously written piece, one part of a three-part series of articles "Going to Canada", appears in *Nieuwsblad van Friesland*, purporting to give trustworthy advice for farm workers. The writer was the Reverend S. A. Schilstra, who happened to be living in the USA. For a couple of years, he was involved with promoting western Canada in a Dutch newspaper.[17] Coincidentally, his article was published during an upturn in social unrest, which culminated in the infamous Spoorwegstaking railway strike on April 6, 1903. The strikers sought the right to organize unions. The government used its military might to suppress the activity of the strikers, particularly in rebellious Amsterdam. The outcome left a atmosphere of mistrust between the government and a large portion of the population, a climate that may have made more people susceptible to the idea of emigration.

From 1905 onward, more specific immigration inducements were circulated, with eye-catching advertisements in Dutch newspapers, such as in *'t Vliegend Blaadje* in Den Helder. In heavy typeset, it touted that about 160 acres of fertile land in Canada was available for each qualified immigrant.[18] Some of these advertisements appear to have been coordinated with interested parties in England. For instance, potential immigrants were directed to inquire at the Dominion of Canada Emigration Office, Charing Cross 11 & 12, or at The Farmers Auxiliary Association, Charing Cross 13, both located in London.

In the large cities in Holland, well-known agencies like Prins & Zwanenberg and Hoymans & Shuurman's which was the agent in Amsterdam for Cunard Line, were also active in immigrant recruitment for Canada. The CPR was represented by Joh. Otten, with offices in both Amsterdam and Rotterdam. This does not mean that the many smaller towns remained untouched by such recruitment efforts. For example, in 1912, J. D. Dijkland, who resided in Heerenveen, was the local agent for Joh. Otten & Zoon[19]. A. van den Berg did likewise through his office at Nonnenveld 421, in Gorinchem.[20] For their efforts the agents were paid "one pound sterling per head" by the Canadian government. The CPR also paid agents for the same services.

Another important agent was The Salvation Army, which became very active in support of emigration in 1907. Through an advertisement in the *Hilversumse Courant*, it aimed to alleviate high unemployment numbers in the towns of Hilversum, Bussum and Baarn.[21] The advertisement mentioned that ships controlled by The Army would leave Rotterdam for Canada on March 12, April 2, April 15, and May 7. Travel expenses for an adult in third class from Rotterdam to the place of landing was 93.80 guilders, which was to be paid by the immigrants themselves. This fee included food: in London, in Liverpool, on the ship, a meal upon arrival, and finally, in a basket for the train journey. In that same year, at least one group of about 150 emigrants left for Canada under the guardianship of the Salvation Army. The Salvation Army's involvement was not without criticism. This humanitarian-focused organization was denounced by some for being paid by the head for each immigrant, as well as for the passages booked.

Advertisement for the Netherlands Transatlantic Mortgage Company 1911, at a store front in Dauphin, Manitoba, circa 1914.

It is impossible to know with any certainty how effective was the distribution of the numerous promotion pamphlets and advertisements in the Dutch newspapers. It is estimated that about 8,000 to 10,000 Dutch immigrants left The Netherlands for Canada between 1900 and 1915. This episode in the history of Dutch immigration to Canada has been examined over the years but, because of the limited numbers of personal records discovered, the picture remains fragmentary and inconclusive. The Dutch, for the most part, emigrated on an individual basis and perhaps were not so inclined to move in organized groups. This diminishes the chance of finding coherent and cohesive records documenting large groups of immigrants. Furthermore, it seems that few records were kept after the settlers had arrived in Canada. For the formal census process, there is no reliable statistical information about their work circumstances or about their daily interactions with Canadian life. "The immigrants have, for the most part, faded into anonymity." [22]

An example of Dutch presence that has completely vanished from the Canadian landscape is that of the numerous Dutch mortgage banks. They were established from 1910 in several locations in the prairie provinces, designed to capitalize on the anticipated stampede of new immigrants. These Dutch banks probably also aimed to attract Dutch immigrants in particular, but undoubtedly welcomed anyone coming through their doors. One such bank was the Nederlandsch-Transatlantische Hypotheekbank (Netherlands Transatlantic Mortgage Company 1911), siting its head office at Winnipeg. To capture clients, the company used advertising like the poster in the window of the store of F.A. Murphy's, auctioneer in Dauphin, Manitoba.

From the available evidence, we can surmise that during the years before World War I the largest concentrations of Dutch immigrants were to be found in larger cities such as Winnipeg, Toronto, and Montreal. The remaining souls were scattered, particularly across western Canada. After Winnipeg received 68 immigrants in 1893, it remained an attractive destination for new immigrants, giving rise to a thriving Dutch community. Smaller communities were established, for instance, at Edam, Saskatchewan and Neerlandia, north of Edmonton, Alberta.

A nucleus of Dutch Catholic immigrants was recruited by the CPR in 1908 specifically for settlement in Strathmore, Alberta. In direct contrast to the favourable images of the already established farms issued by the CPR through pamphlets and other media, these immigrants' initial encounters with farming in Canada were harrowing experiences. The extremely bad weather of 1908 disrupted the sugar beet harvest and forced a number of men to leave — their only other option was to undertake backbreaking labour in the forests of British Columbia. Despite the ordeal of these men, the CPR continued to recruit additional immigrants for the Strathmore project. In November of 1908, it was announced in the newspaper that Emile Wustefeld of Zutphen, The Netherlands had become an agent for Canadian Pacific's Irrigation Colonization Department in Calgary to pursue further recruitment[23] of immigrants.

During this period, the Canadian economy could not accommodate its rapidly increasing workforce. Canadian cities were faced with high unemployment. In Toronto, Dutch immigrants came knocking at the door of the Dutch consul for assistance. Negative news about the acute unemployment situation in Canada appeared in various Dutch newspapers. According to the February 16, 1908 edition of *De Rijnbode*, a young shoemaker, knowledgeable in farming skills, wrote to his mother that after a year of searching he had still not found a good job. To survive, he had taken a job where he had to sleep with 40 folks in a bitterly cold and smoky shack, with a plank for a bed and only one blanket. His story is that while working on a steam shovel, several accidents happened and one soul lost his head. No one seemed to care. Sunday was a workday and if one refused to work, the job was gone. The article went on to report that Dutch immigrants did return to Toronto but there were already thousands of unemployed there. The article ends with the words "we have been deceived and the consul has taken an interest in our plight".[24] Such articles, along with the alarming information received from the Dutch consul in Toronto, forced the Dutch Minister of Foreign Affairs to respond by placing notices in the Dutch newspapers. The notices were designed to discourage some and advise others to wait before emigrating to Canada, so long as this bad situation continued.

Around the same time as these actions were taken by the Dutch government, apparently contradictory newspaper articles were written. On one hand, office workers and the like were urged not to emigrate, but on the other hand, promotional materials still continued to appear asking for farmers, tradesmen and domestic aids who ostensibly would find work without encountering too much difficulty. News about these negative briefings had also reached Canada. To rebut the negative press, J. H. Kooimans from Nakusp, British Columbia wrote in *Het Nieuws van den Dag* of May 25, 1908 that he was surprised to hear about it. He said that Nakusp was a lovely place where 15 Hollanders lived and anybody who wanted to immigrate should do so, especially those with money. That would, of course, he continued, give them a head-start — they could buy a "fruit–farm". He wrote that there was also work for labourers whose wages were, on average, higher than in other provinces where the minimum wage was $2.00 a day. [25]

Being exposed to mixed messages (from beating the drum for emigration to discouraging it) must have exacerbated the struggle to make the decision to leave the Netherlands. In the end, Dutch people, from all walks of life, in pursuit of a different life, ignored the warnings from their government and others. They pressed on and continued to put down stakes in Canada, some following family members or friends, or perhaps seeking places where Dutch folks had already settled. One of the many who did just that was Henk van Elst, a former lineman of the telegraph company and a citizen from Amersfoort. He must have believed the positive messages by Kooiman because in 1913 he joined other Dutch immigrants in Nakusp.[26]

The Dutch continued to immigrate to the Granum-Monarch-Nobleford area, located in Southern Alberta.

Fortunately and with thanks to thorough research by Donald Sinnema, we know much more about the fate of the cluster of immigrants who settled there between 1903–1914. His book is based on letters written by the immigrants which had been published in various Dutch newspapers. Sinnema covers the movements of this small group of immigrants who were raised in the Reformed tradition, belonging to a more conservative protestant sector of Dutch society.[27]

In order to come to a broader understanding and gain some personal insights, more research about Dutch immigration is needed. However, according to historian, Dr. Herman Ganzevoort, research on Dutch emigration faces serious obstacles. Attempts to reconstruct events and circumstances in the intimate lives of emigrants are difficult, especially due to the deficiency of personal records, most of which, for whatever reason, apparently have not survived.[28]

Fortuitously, the relatively small collection in this book consists of some personal records that did survive. It helps us remember and honour some hardy individuals, and gives voice to their experiences — the very antithesis of anonymity. Furthermore, it counters a generally accepted image of the poor, uneducated, ignorant immigrant. Instead, we see surprisingly broad diversity, in their backgrounds, levels of education, interests and capabilities.

The Voices

"The human voice is
the organ of the soul."
— Henry Woodsworth Longfellow

It is not a big stretch to suggest that a commonly-held belief is that the largest contingent of Dutch immigrants must have been working-class people. After all, they were supposed to gain economically by starting a new life in Canada. For people sitting firmly in the saddle, money was not necessarily the driver — they could have simply been thirsty for adventure.

We cannot know the exact makeup of the Dutch immigrant population but these postcards suggest that Dutch immigrants did not make up a homogeneous group of people. They were from all walks of life — yes, the working class in cities and on the land, but also the middle class, the self-employed, and tradespeople. Still a few more were professionals or members of the upper class and nobility.

For example, there was Cornelis Olree who was a working-class painter and his wife, Pieternella Johanna Olree-de Moor from Zeeland. Compare Olree's background with that of Jean Alexandre, Jonkheer van Hoogenhouck Tulleken, a member of the Dutch nobility, who settled in Toronto around 1900 and became a businessman. Yet another segment of Dutch society, the upper middle class, is represented by Alphonse Caspar Marie Muysken, a son of a military officer from Sas van Gent as Muysken. Then there is Jan Lodewijk Waller, who was from the financial upper class, which was mostly centered in Amsterdam. He immigrated to Canada around 1900 and married a Canadian, Clara May Bull on September 21, 1904 in Winnipeg.

For almost a century, their voices and the voices of the other authors have fallen silent. In the following chapters, their voices will emerge from late 19th and early 20th century Canada through an array of different messages on the postcards. For many reasons it was impossible to trace all identities and backgrounds of the senders and receivers. Nevertheless, they all had something in common. They sent postcards to The Netherlands at particular times from particular places to inform the folks at home about their emotional and physical situations in their new country, Canada, and to remind those at 'home' that they were still in their thoughts and hearts.

Collectively, they share the themes of arriving in the new country, of becoming established. They share their new surroundings and they send condolences. They just say "hi" and they celebrate milestones like marriages and the birth of a child. Many express the anguish of losing contact and the need to hear from home. Moreover, they share the most difficult decisions, not the least of which is whether to stay in their new country or to return home. This book follows these themes and shows that regardless of the origins of the immigrant, their connections to the homeland remained important to them.

Early Days

The first chapter starts at the beginning — arrival in Canada.

Saying goodbye to their place of birth was the first hurdle for the new immigrants. The next was to find their way to one of the large Dutch ports. In many cases, they took a ship on the first leg of their monumental journey to a port in Great Britain. From there, they set sail on an ocean liner.

Upon arrival in Canada, the passengers had to find their way to their final destination. For some, this meant enduring a long and exhausting trip through endless countryside by railway.

Their immediate notes to the old country suggest relief at a safe crossing, excited anticipation of what is to come, and first impressions of their new country.

One of the many immigrants that took this route was Andries Klass Doedenias Meeter (born August 4, 1885, in The Hague). He married Beatrice Ellen Boutilier on December 22, 1919 in Halifax. She was born April 2, 1881. He was a bookkeeper by profession. Meeter sailed from Liverpool on the *R.M.S. Alsatian* of the Allan Line to Halifax. The ship was a 18,481 gross-ton ship that had accommodation for 287 first class, 504 second class, and 848 third class passengers. This postcard which he mailed home shows the Alsatian, which was built in Glasgow in 1913.

He wrote from the ship on April 16, 1914 about his expected arrival in Halifax. It must have been an anxious time for him, being so close to Canada's shores. Perhaps these feelings were shared by other immigrants on the 3rd class deck, which Meeter had marked at the stern with an 'X'.

The card was mailed by Andries K.D. Meeter to his father, Doedenias Meeter in The Hague from the ship and postmarked April 16, 1914, Halifax, Nova Scotia. At that time, his father was a retired civil servant.

"X Third class deck"

Dear Everyone,
Thursday morning.

We will arrive tomorrow after 12:00 in Halifax. When I am at my destination, I shall tell of my adventures in a long letter. There is no paper and not even envelopes. Completely well. Cozy on board.

Many greetings, Andries

Greetings from Canada

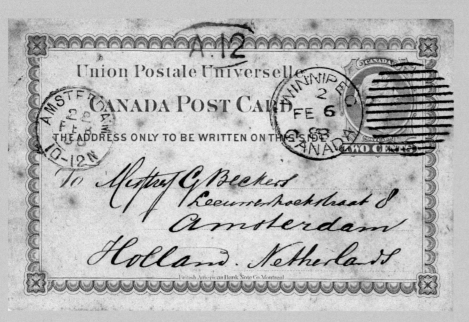

This card was mailed by Johannes C. van 't Hull to his step father, Mr. Gerardus Beckers, from Winnipeg to Amsterdam on February 6, 1888.
Johannes C. van 't Hull, born in 1855 in Nijmegen, was a wine merchant in Gorinchem where his father was the Police Commissioner. He was married there on August 13, 1874 to Helen S. B. Boonzajer. It is not known how long van 't Hull remained in Canada or when he eventually travelled to the United States, as his obituary refers to him as residing in St. Paul Minnesota by 1892.

Dear Sir,

Finally the chest arrived in Winnipeg. I can pick it up at one o'clock after having endured all kinds of formalities about which I will write to you. It is now 12 o'clock and since I am at the post office I have let you already know about the arrival.

t.a.t. [tout à toi, or 'all to you'] J. C. van 't Hull

PRIVATE POST CARD.

THIS SPACE MAY BE USED
FOR CORRESPONDENCE

Geliefde Zuster
over eenige dagen
zend ik je een letter
of liever groote brief
ik krijg goed werk hier
in Canada ik ben
met het leger des
Heils gekomen

THIS SPACE IS FOR ADDRESS ONLY

Miss G. Langerveld
adres Mr G Klein
in fancy articles
Meppel
Holland

This card was mailed from Montreal, Quebec, April 1907 to Grietje Langerveld, in Meppel.

She was the author's sister, who, at the time, lived and worked in a 'fancy articles' shop owned by A. Klein. Grietje was born on June 24, 1880 on her father's ship moored in the Achterzaan te Zaandam. In 1911, she married Johannes Jacobs, also from Zaandam.

Dear Sister,

In a few days, I will mail you a letter, or rather a large letter. I got good work in Canada, and I came with the Salvation Army.

Dear Mr. and Mrs.,

Hereby, I am letting you know that I arrived in Montreal in good health.

There were several Dutchmen on board and we had a good time. My husband was happy that I came home, and was mad at the child.

Thanking you for everything,

Mrs. Van Haarsbergen

The card was mailed from Montreal, Quebec to Mr. van Leeuwen at a hat store in Rotterdam on October 24, 1912.

Dear Family Kraak!

I am happy to have arrived in Toronto and hope to write a long letter about my journey, soon. I can tell you already that, except the two days I was seasick, the journey was successful. "A" wrote to me that she had a few comfortable days with you, which I can well imagine.

Many Greetings from your loving Catharina

320 College Street, Toronto, Ontario, Canada

The "Grange," Home of the Late Prof. Goldwin Smith, Toronto, Canada

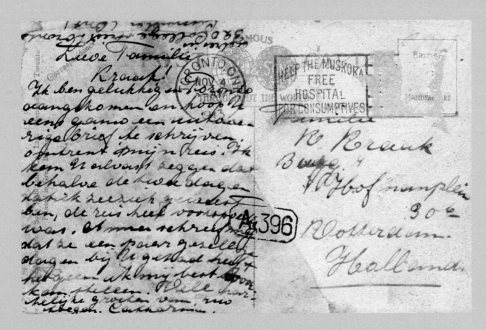

This card was mailed on November 4, 1913 to K. Kraak, an office clerk in Rotterdam.

This card was mailed on May 1, 1914 from Toronto, Ontario to Maria van der Zweep-Vlaming in Winterswijk. Maria was married to Cesar (Co) van der Zweep on June 1, 1911, in Utrecht. Ietje (Ina) was her daughter. Co was a clerk at the Hollandsche IJzeren Spoorweg-Maatschappij. Kal could be her brother Klaas.

Dominion Bank, Toronto, Canada

Dear Maria:

We have arrived safely, but three days behind schedule, still we are with people who had walked for three days to the railway station. Now Mari you will also sometimes hear from me. Say "Hello" to Co and Ietje and from all of us, also "Hello".

From your loving Kal
Grantstreet 28

123.- C. P. R. Subway, Winnipeg.

Dear Brother and Sister!

*I am hereby letting you know
that I have arrived in Canada,
all right. I had a good journey
but it is here still very cold and
snow is falling. I like the city but
I cannot say much. I have to be
here a bit longer.*

*With all my regards
Your brother
J Rietman
28/3 '08*

This card showing the C.P.R.
subway in Winnipeg was
mailed on March 30, 1908,
from Winnipeg, Manitoba to
Aalderikus Mooi, a carpenter in
Winschoten.

9

Assiniboine Park, Winnipeg, Man.

The card was sent from Winnipeg, Manitoba to Mieke van Marle, March 28, 1911 in Hilversum.

Dear Mieke:

You see we arrived in good order. We had a lot of storm but we did not get seasick. The cold weather turns out to be better than anticipated and there is no snow thus things will go all right. Anton has been operated on. He had a lump in his stomach. The doctor does not know what kind of lump it is. His situation is according to the last information very good. All the best greeting from all of us and do write back soon.
Your loving friend,
A. Kooijman.

Our address is Louis Bridge, Manitoba, Canada

Cornelis Antonie (Antoon) Kooijman was born May 4, 1854 in Vianen and passed away March 12, 1934, Winnipeg.

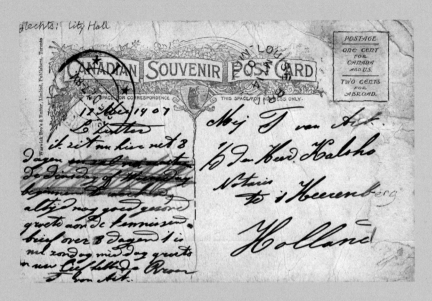

This card *(left)* was mailed on May 12, 1907 from Louise Bridge, Manitoba to Teuntje van Ark in 's-Heerenberg. Van Ark was born August 7, 1880 in Heerde.

12 May 1907

Dear Sister:

I am here just 3 days and will start working the eighteenth Tuesday or Wednesday.
I am still very healthy, greetings to the acquaintances. Letter over 8 days. It is now Sunday afternoon.

Teunis van Dijk was born September 2, 1890 in Amerongen. His father was Arie van Dijk and his mother was Dirkje Lucassen.

Greetings for now.
Your loving brother,
T. van Ark

Dear Sister:

I shall just write you something. Up to now everything goes well. I have arrived in Winnipeg at 5:30 a.m. and leave again at 3:30 p.m. I think to be in C. on Tuesday evening.

The best regards from your brother. Teunis

This card was mailed on April 14, 1912 from Winnipeg, Manitoba to Amerongen.

Dalls Rapids, Winnipeg, Man.

This card was mailed from Winnipeg on March 27, 1912 to Mr. Jan Bakker in Amsterdam.

Have a few more days of patience and then I will be able to mail my permanent address to you.

All is fine.
Bertus

This card is signed 'Marc', and was likely mailed by Marcus Rühmann (later of Strathmore). It went to Bernardus Henrikus ten Raa, an office clerk, and his wife Maria Elisabeth ten Raa-Freund in Amsterdam. ten Raa-Freund, born on September 20, 1869 in Amsterdam, is likely the sister of Rühmann's wife, Anna Elisabeth.

Dear Brother and Sister-in-law,

I arrived here on Thursday and I hope all is well with you . . .

Yours, Marc

Court-House, Winnipeg   Notman, Photo

This card was mailed by Cornelis Olree on May 3, 1907 from Calgary, Alberta to Souburg.

Dear Friend,

We have arrived in Calgary where we now have to wait. I just met a Dutchman there, a bricklayer from Utrecht. Then we went into the city. Letter will follow. We are going to Camrose.

Many greetings from
C. Olree and P. Olree

Cornelis Olree, a painter, was born August 30, 1873 in Middelburg and Pieternella Johanna de Moor, his wife was born October 15, 1877 in Axel.

Strathmore 4. 11

Receive today the news of my good arrival. Everybody healthy? Otherwise, greetings from your nephew…

Address is c/o Mr. M. A. Pals, farmer, Strathmore, Box 35, Alta., Canada, NA

Martin Pals's family with five children came in 1909 from Princenhage to Strathmore. They farmed NW 1/4 of S-29, T-24, R-24,W of 4th. All except the oldest daughter, Dena, moved to Castor in 1914, where the family still farms.

This card was mailed from Strathmore, Alberta on April 16, 1911 to Theodorus M.F.M. Siegmund in Breda. Siegmund was a sport instuctor at the Royal Miltary Academy (KMA) in Breda.

Arrived safely in Halifax. We go further by train, and are already sitting 24 hours in the train. Because of being very busy, I am writing this card in the train.

Many greetings of the family,
S. de Ruijter.

This card was mailed by H.J.A. Simons de Ruijter on May 2, 1907 from Montreal to Lina Jansen in Amsterdam.

HALIFAX, N.S. FROM THE CITADEL.

Hendrikus Jacobus Albertus Simons de Ruijter was born October 20, 1860 in Augsbuurt, Friesland, the son of a pastor. He worked as a clerk for a South African railway, at least until 1901. In May 1907, he emigrated from the Netherlands with his family, settling in Winnipeg at 111 Inkster Avenue. He started a business 'de Ruyter and Humsfeld', also in Winnipeg, at 518 Ashdown Block, the nature of which is unknown. One year later, he returned to Holland. He held various posts with organizations devoted to social issues, as the treasurer of the Beth-Pallet, an organization to support unmarried mothers and their children, and as a member of the Armenraad, a group established to advise to the City of Amsterdam on improving the lot of the poor. In addition, he served with Rijksbureau tot bestrijding van den handel in vrouwen (National Office to eliminate the trade in women) for which he was awarded the honorary title of Commissarus van de Rijkspolitie (Commissioner of the National Police). He died in Amsterdam, February 20, 1924.

2

Reassurances and Health

This card was mailed by Dirk Kroes on December 12, 1911 from Preston, Ontario to his sister Antje Kroes at the Diaconessenhuis (hospital) in Haarlem.

Dear Sister,

Hereby, I am letting you know that we have received your letter today in good health, but how long it will take, we don't know, because it is here already time. We were surprised to find out that you were laying in the hospital and that is awful. We hope that you get better very soon and do not worry about that apron. Many greetings from your brother and his wife.
Write soon.

Dirk Kroes, age 21, arrived in Quebec on May 20, 1907 aboard the *Southwark*. He was a carpenter and he married Mary Adeline Levan in Preston on December 23, 1908.

This card was mailed from an illegible location, beginning with 'North', to Marten van der Geest in Schiermonnikoog. He was born May 7, 1858 in Schiermonnikoog, married to Milania Mechielsen, born March 23, 1884 in Schiermonnikoog. They are Petrus' parents.

Dear Father!

I can inform you that I am still healthy and I hope you are also healthy. It is a bit cold here and it snows off and on.

Well, greetings from your son
P. J. v d G. 38 bourg [place of origin is illegible]

Petrus J. van der Geest was born July 6, 1888 in Schiermonnikoog. On June 10, 1916 in Kollumerland, he married Aaltje Heins (b. June 13, 1888 in Kollum).

Along the Elbow River, Calgary, Alta

This card was mailed on May 19, 1915 from Calgary, Alberta to Dr. M. Kievit in Bathmen who died at the age of 67 on September 2, 1935.

Many greetings from the new country, as they call it here. The climate here is lovely, but we recently had a layer of snow. I feel very good and have had no problems with my stomach.

With many greetings,
Mrs. van der Borch.

This is probably Albertine Pauline Jeane Francoise Baroness van Hardenbroek van Lockhorst who was married to Reinier Charles Paul Henri Baron van der Borch. They lived in Bathmen until 1911.

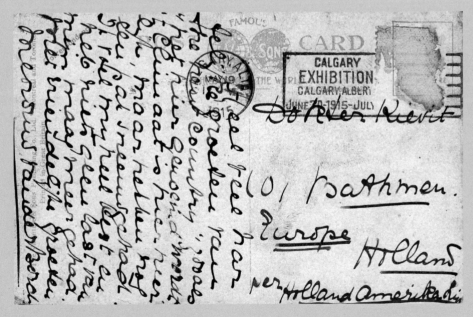

Greetings from Canada

Dear Maartje,

Receive this text in healthy circumstances. We are luckily very well, only a bit much on the toilet but that is better than to be crazy. How are you doing? Wish to your mother and everyone else, many greetings. How is your mother doing, has she stayed all right? I hope, yes. Oh Maartje, it was very cold here, but while I write this card it is mild weather the whole day, but in general it is cold. I hope that it will be milder soon. We can still make it nicely warm, here. Maartje, has Johan received Piets card? . . . The children are very good. Piet can still remember you very well. And he won't forget you, he says. Say hello to everybody, also to your Sister.

Receive now the many greetings from your loving sister, Anna-many greetings from H. van Maarten-Kwakkelstein

This card was mailed from Montreal, Quebec on February 3, 1914 to Maartje Kwakkelstein in Vlaardingen. At this address lived the family of Hendrik Kwakkelstein who was born January 24, 1847 in Vlaardingen. He was a factory worker and married to Kornelia Kwakkelstein-de Goede, born March 10, 1850 in Vlaardingen. Among their children was Maartje, born November 2, 1889 in Vlaardingen.

Montreal   Winter on Mount Royal.

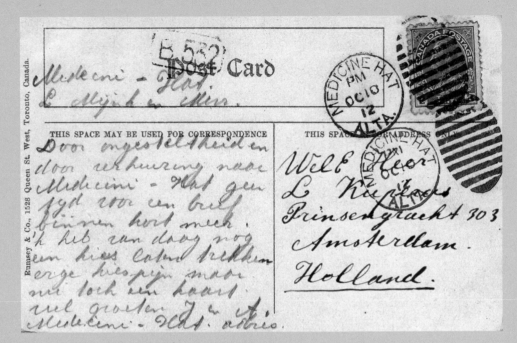

Dear Mr. and Mrs.,

Due to sickness and due to moving to Medicine Hat, I had no time for a letter. Soon more. I had a tooth extracted today after a terrible toothache, but still, a card.

Many greetings. J & A

This card was mailed by Jan and Anna (surname unknown) from Medicine Hat, Alberta on October 10, 1912 to Mr. Luitjen Kuperus in Amsterdam. Kuperus, an elementary school teacher, was born on June 27, 1861 in Wildervank. On May 17, 1888, he married Alida Johanna Kropholler, born on March 27, 1849 in Amsterdam.

City Hall, Medicine Hat, Alta, Canada

This card was mailed by Jan Pieter Klomp from Fort Williams, Ontario on November 20, 1907 to Willem Truijens, a former employer, in Amsterdam. Truijens was born March 19, 1886 in Zwaag.

Klomp was born on April 3, 1880 in Haarlemermeer.

Boss Truijens,

With this card I can inform you that I am still very healthy, hoping the same for you and the whole family. A short while ago I received a letter from home and also greetings from you. My sister also wrote me that I can expect a letter from you. I hope you keep your word. Do you have work this summer? Or does it not matter? I still work at my first boss. And how are things with your wife? Still healthy? I hope yes, also for Nico and your other sons and daughters. Let me honour you by bringing you a cup of tea? And now Boss Truijens, greetings to the acquaintances and the best greetings for your family and you is also being wished by someone who came to Canada, and who is called the Canadian.

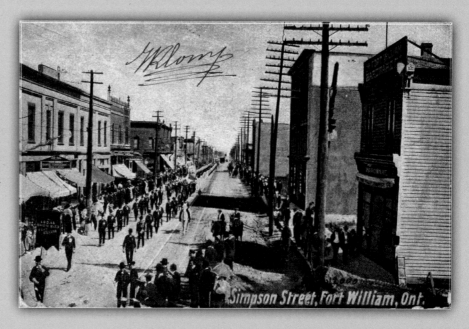

This card was sent from Chesley, Ontario May 19, 1913 to Amsterdam.

Dear Pastor,

Because of serious sickness of my wife, we forgot to write. We are doing fine and for six dollars a month we live in a nice house with a large garden with five fruit trees. I hope that you are also doing fine. I wrote Guus a card to Wapenveld and I am very anxious to receive a return letter for the first time.

Many Greetings, R.E. Schwars and . . .

This card was mailed from Edmonton, Alberta on August 3, 1911 to the Reverend B. F. van Maas in Wapenveld. van Maas was born January 17, 1866 in Haarlem and passed away February 16, 1918 in Apeldoorn, from the Spanish flu. In Wapenveld, there is a school that carries his name.

I am still in good health. The natural surroundings are here like in Holland. All roads like this road on the card are country roads. It is beautiful to walk here. Making a wage goes well. Also I make 2.25 dollars a day.

Your student, J.W. Galis.

Dear Parents and brother,

Presently I am in Nakusp, where I am working with some other Dutchmen. For the moment I board at the house of the family Funcke , who have lived in Amersfoort at the threepoint. I received last week your picture postcard but have not received a word from Jacob, as yet. I hope to hear from him soon. How are you all doing? Has mother improved? I hope yes. We all are also in good very health.

Greetings from your son and brother, Henk. Bye!

Henk was born Hendrik van Elst, c. 1885, in Waardenburg. He was a telegraph lineman. He was married to Cornelia Hermina de Gans who was born April 26, 1884 in Amersfoort. They were married on September 22, 1908 in Amersfoort. He passed away in 1967.

This card was mailed from Nakusp, British Columbia on November 11, 1913 to his father, Hermanus van Elst, postman, in Amersfoort.

Nakusp, Arrow Lakes, B.C.

3

Making a Living

Your Honour, Mr. Gerlings,

Your letter, etc., has been received. I am happy to hear that London is doing well and that the trees grow so nicely. Many thanks for the information. We are very busy at the brewery, first for Christmas, now for "le jour de l'ander". Frenchmen—thank God they drink a lot, especially on holidays. I trust that your health is all right.

Receive my best wishes for the New Year.

This card was mailed from Montreal, Quebec on December 30, 1897 to J.D. Oortman Gerlings in Utrecht.

Preston, Canada.   From Water Tower.

This card was mailed on November 26, 1912 from Preston, Ontario to Spaarndam.

At the moment it is winter because the snow is high and it is very cold. You would not venture outside. Today I have to do some roofing with zinc layers. It is cold work because the snow is also on the roof. You have to clean the roof first and a half hour later the roof is covered again. It is a job that is cold but I can handle it.

Greetings from
W. de Vries

W. de Vries, age 19, arrived on September 9, 1905 aboard the *Virginian* at Quebec.

Greetings from Canada

This card was mailed by Simon Bais from Elbow, Saskatchewan on March 4, 1915 to his parents, Cornelis Bais and Henriette Sophia Bais-Dersjant. Cornelis was a baker in Heemstede.

Dear Parents,

The four of us are staying a week with the former boss of Simon. Later on we will write more about it.

For now, from here, our many greetings. Marie, Truus, Simon, Dick

Simon Bais, born 15 June, 1890 in Amsterdam, died February 7, 1954 in Winnipeg. His wife Marie van der Drift, born 25 February 1886 in Leiden, died October 13, 1949 in Winnipeg. They were married on 27 June, 1915 in Winnipeg.

Carrying Grain to the Elevators, Saskatchewan, Canada

This card was mailed by Sjoerd Brongersma on June 12, 1911 from Cupar, Saskatchewan to Verlengde Schans near Leeuwarden.

Dear Friends!

How are you both? Very healthy? Can you see that this is one of our farmhands? With a seeding machine. Mother has most likely told you everything about my travel journey. I like to live here very much. We have a nice house and a large garden. We live close to the road. Of course, here is not as much activity as in Schans, and there are not as much pensioners walking in the morning as by you. Everything looks promising here. Sjoerd has not written your son yet. Writing, that is a quite a job. We are busy during the day and then it never goes beyond the planning. Do you have also news about him?

Receive our amicable greetings,
Sjoerd en Wytske

Sjoerd (Samuel) and Wytske arrived in 1900 in Canada. Sjoerd was born February 27, 1879 and his sister Wytske June 29, 1881, both in Leeuwarden. They farmed near Cupar. SE 1/4 S-36, T-23, R-17, W of 2nd.

This card was mailed from Strathmore, Alberta in 1911, to Miss C. Hermans in Roosendaal.

Dear Cristie,

I hereby send you another card. I will soon write a long letter. Do not be mad that I have waited so long. There was no time during the harvest. Thank God that came through successfully.
You should sometime, perhaps, inquire after Mr. Corstman, who has visited me.

Best greetings from all of us, Cor.

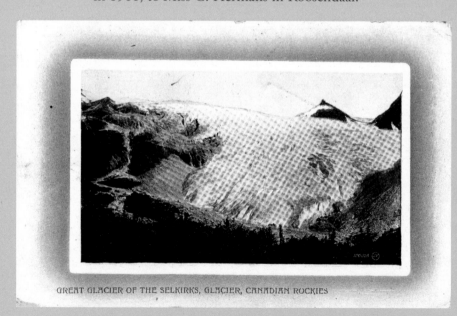

GREAT GLACIER OF THE SELKIRKS, GLACIER, CANADIAN ROCKIES

This card was mailed from Toronto by A. Eikenaar on June 13, 1907 to Arie van Randeraat in Amsterdam.

This card was mailed from North Battleford, Saskatchewan on 1908 to Miss Sina Elbers in Hengelo.

Dear Friend,

I finally got around to fulfilling my promise. I have arrived here all right, after having experienced many adventures. I have a good job at a large car factory. The wage in our trade is here 25 cents [pounds sterling], 62.5 cents Can. an hour. Toronto is a large city of about 300,000 inhabitants, in area, larger than Amsterdam. I start to feel at home here already. There is all over an abundance of work. How are you doing at the Handelsblad [newspaper] and how is your car? Please say hello to your family and the acquaintances at the Algemeen Handelsblad.

Many greetings from your friend, A. Eikenaar.

In the Toronto City Directory of 1912 A. Eikenaar is listed as living at Thos. agt, house 1371, Dundas.

From us—G. T. Mars. Post Office
N. Battleford, Sask., Canada

Dear Sister,

We are here, still very healthy, I also hope the same for you. I am a server in the hotel but that, you have already heard from our mother. Many thanks for your portrait, I like it very much. G works for himself, he builds a small house with another Hollander and we will see later how things will go. Our boys have not written to you, they have been ailing but they are now healthy again. It is very warm here—later more news. G. will again become a butcher for $50 a month and later still more.

Greetings for all and please write us.
Greetings from your Sister H, and G.

Greetings from Canada

This card was mailed from Edmonton on August 12, 1913 to the 'Family Huybregts' in Scheveningen.

Dear Grandmother,

I now have a job in a small hotel. I worked for one day in a large restaurant, but because I could not understand the head waitress, who had a Canadian dialect, and since I don't speak good English, I was let go. I don't earn much but when I speak the language better, I can ask for more.

I hope to get a letter from home, soon, to hear how you are all doing. How is the weather in Scheveningen? It is very hot here. Have you been able to rent the rooms?

Adieu. Many greetings to everybody.

Have you received the cards?

This card was probably enclosed in an envelope in December of 1907. It was addressed "Winnipeg, Manitoba" and sent to Johannes Jacobus Hopmans, born October 18, 1865, a coffee shop owner in Naarden. This is near Bussem where Scheffer and Peter van Zanten, referred to in his card, were from. van Zanten (a painter) was born September 22, 1872 in Weesp, would emigrate with his wife and four children to Minneapolis, Minnesota, USA.

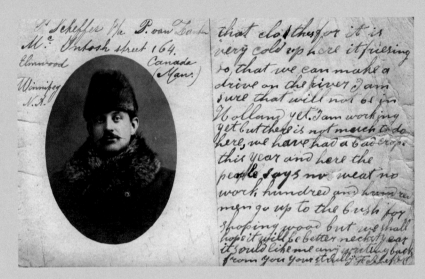

Dear Friend and Misses,

I wish you a Happy New Year and many returns of it, and I hope you will expect this in a good health. I am very well, too. Well how do you like that portrait? It is like a Prussian isn't it? Everybody wants those clothes for it is very cold up here. It is freezing so that we can drive on the river. I am sure that will not be so in Holland yet. I am still working but there is not much to do here. We have had a bad crop this year and here the people say "no wheat, no work". Hundreds and hundreds of men go up to the bush for chopping wood but we shall hope it will be better next year. I would like you to write back to me.

Yours truly, F. Scheffer.
F. Scheffer c/o P. van Zanten, McIntosh street 164, Elmwood, Winnipeg, Canada (Man.) N.A.

This is probably Fransiscus Scheffer, aged 37, who arrived in Quebec on May 2, 1907 aboard the *Athena*.

Royal Alexandria Hospital, Edmonton, Alberta

This card was probably mailed within an envelope.

We will make clear in a letter why you should write to Ytze. We are all healthy. At the moment I work in the coal mines.

There is big money made and I am therefore free of the war.

Ytze Bankert, age 27, arrived with Cornelis, age 2, and Martze, aged 5 months, in Quebec, November 10, 1907 aboard the *Southwark*.

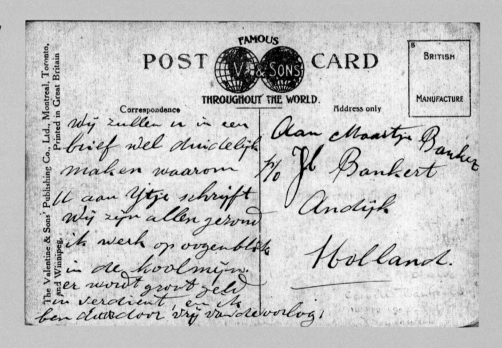

This card was mailed by Jacob P. Boon on March 5, 1907 from Regina, Saskatchewan to the legendary banking institution, Ranzow en Co., in Arnhem.

Dear Sir,

While thanking you, I can tell you that the other letter with the same content has arrived in good order.

Thanking you again for your assistance.

Remaining yours faithfully,

J.P. Boon
Riverview P.O., Davidson, Sask. Canada

Please pay end of 106[?]
Y. in haste

Robbert

20/May

The card was mailed by Robbert Insinger on May 21, 1893 from Yorkton, Assiniboina to Insinger & Javaansche Bank in Amsterdam.

Frederik Robbert Insinger was born in Brummen, December 6, 1862, into a wealthy family. This bank was owned by members of Robbert Insinger's family.

He immigrated to Canada in 1885 and settled near Yorkton, Saskatchewan (at that time part of the Northwest Territories) where he started ranching (NW S-32, T-25, R-6, W of 2nd).

He became a member of the Legislative Assembly of the Northwest Territories first representing the constituency of Wallace from 1892–1894 and later the Yorkton constituency from 1894 to 1897.

The town of Insinger, Saskatchewan is named in his honour.

Dear Family Brandhoff,

At present I can inform you that we are in Saskatoon. This coming Monday, A will start working. I work as a carpenter for a Dutchman where we are boarding. Is it not crazy — me a carpenter? Still, it is true and I make 27–28 cents an hour and work 8–9 hours a day. A good carpenter makes here 40 or 45 cents an hour. The wages here are good. Later on I shall write you more.

Many greetings from Anna and me.
J.G.J. van Nes

This card was mailed from Saskatoon, Saskatchewan on March 26, 1912 to Johannes Brandhoff, a carpenter in Bussum.

This card was mailed on June 10, 1911 by Hendrik Willem Ovink, from Preston, Ontario to A. Van de Ven in Arnhem.

Dear Friend,

I have good work here and earn more than 30 dollars per week and if I can speak the language better, I will get more. There is work in abundance here, but the English language that is weak. They must point everything to me. When everything has improved, you will get a letter.

H. W. Ovink

Ovink was born on May 15, 1865 in Gaanderen. He was a painter by profession and was married to Wilhelmina Hendrika Hentzepeter.

Marriage, Birth, Mourning

4

Approach to Victoria Bridge. Grand Trunk Railway, Montreal.

This card was mailed by Eremina "Mina" Lammerts van Bueren in Montreal, Quebec on July 28, 1910 to her cousin Cornelia Lammerts van Bueren in Ginneken. Mina, her sister, Marie, and her widowed mother, Louise, lived at 34 Lorne Ave. in Montreal.

My dear Corrie,

We are anxious to know how Aunt Mie is keeping after this sore trial of . . . dear sister taken away from you dear, who have now to shoulder all the burden alone. It would be yet less trying if you were perfectly well. There is no one can take your place in that home. Even should one of our cousins come, it is true they might relieve you of some of the household duties. May God give you strength to bear up. I was so pleased to hear from you that Aunt Kee loved her saviour that she is now waiting for the rest of her . . . dear ones. Please send me a word to let me know how you are all.

Your loving cousin, Mina.

Jonkheer Jean Alexandre van Hoogenhouck Tulleken was born in Batavia, May 25, 1873. He married Frances Lilian Dignam on January 11, 1901 in Toronto. She was born in London, Ontario, December 29, 1880. In 1924, Tulleken, a Reserve Major and businessman, built a large house, named *Ceederheem* at 6 Plymbridge Road in Toronto. He died January 11, 1940.

Amice.

By this card I am informing you about my forth- coming wedding, which will take place on coming June 1. I appeal politely to all the interested parties to regard this information as if it were personally directed to each of them. Adieu.

With a heartfelt handshake,
T.A.T. [tout à toi, or 'all to you'] Tulleken

This card was mailed on May 22, 1901 from Yorkville, Ontario to Anthonius Adrianus Fredericus Quant in Leiden. Quant was born February 8, 1849 in Leiden.

Tulleken used a card with a stamp from the Woman's Art Association of Canada, which was founded in 1886.

View at Saskatoon, Sask.

Dear Jacob and Lucie, I personally wanted to congratulate you on your marriage, the most significant event in our human life. With all my heart I hope that you will be really happy together and that the sun might shine upon your lives and in case darkness shows up, think than about the sentence, "Let open the door, let in the sun, She has a smile for everyone". I hope that you have received the papers in time. I am anxious to know when the wedding day is. Receive my wishes and also from Jan for the New Year. "A Merry Christmas and a Happy New Year." Please convey my greetings to Lucie, Mother and sisters. I congratulate them also regarding your wedding. Many kisses for Beppie and Jantje, also most friendly embraced by your loving Jan and Betsy. Also congratulations with your terrific appointment. Good that things are going so well with you.

Bye, Jacob and Lucie.
Goodbye Jan and Betsy

This card was mailed from Saskatoon, Saskatchewan on December 21, 1914 to Jacob Faiwusch Rabinowitsch and his wife Lucia Gerarda Rabinowitsch-van Bijleveldt in Heerenveen. Both were born in Amsterdam. Jacob was appointed on September 30, 1914 to become a German language teacher at the high school (HBS) in Heerenveen.

This card was mailed on September 14, 1913 from Winnipeg, Manitoba to the family Dirk Franken. Franken was a commercial agent in Haarlem, born on September 18, 1886 in Schoten.

Dear Family!

Finally has the time arrived that I can announce that I was married on the 16th of August. I had a good trip. At the first opportunity I shall write you a letter. That I waited so long to inform you and others is that after my husband had recuperated, I ended up in the hospital. I am now also completely recuperated and my plan is to write soon to Holland. So please do not hold it against me that I am so late to inform you.

Greetings to both of you.

From . . .

The return address refers to Berend Voorsmit, who does not appear to be the writer of the card. He is listed in the 1913 Henderson's Directory for Winnipeg as being a cook in the Olympia Café.

Voorsmit was born September 1, 1881 in Groningen. He later lived in Kamsack, Saskatchewan.

The card was mailed by Daniel F. Boissevain on September 29, 1884 from Brandon, Manitoba to his sister Emma Julia Henriette Boissevain, at Hilversum.

Dearest E.

Just received, after coming home, the extremely distressing intelligence of our beloved father's most serious illness. (Letters dated 8.10 and 12). I hope to write tomorrow night. This just to let you know that I am now grieving with you and in great anxiety.

God's will be done, your affectionate Brother, DFB
Daniel Boissevain

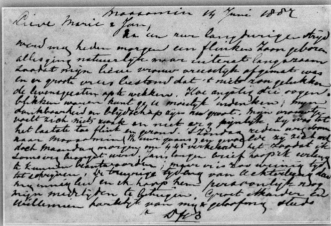

This card was mailed by Daniel Boissevain on June 14, 1887 from Moosmin, Northwest Territories to Werkhoven, to his sister Marie and his brother-in-law, the Jonhkeer Jan van Beeck Calkoen.

Dear Marie and Jan,

After a very long struggle, this morning, a sizeable son was born. Everything of course went very slowly so that my dear wife was terribly tired and we were afraid that it not would be possible to revive her. It is difficult to imagine how anxious those moments were. My thankfulness and happiness are very great now. My wife does not feel weak and is not in pain. She was until the last moment spirited and healthy. Sunday, we had driven to Moosamin (about 1½ hour drive) and she felt well. However, Monday morning at 4:25 things went wrong, which made me anxious off and on. I hope to soon answer Jan's long letter; but there is so little time for writing. The sad news about . . . and I hope still to express my personal condolences to him.

Say hello to Xander and Willemien many greetings from me and believe in me for ever,
DFB

Marett Burridge Boissevain, the child referred to in this card, was born Tuesday, June 14, 1887 in Cannington Manor, N.W.T. His father and the author of this card, Daniel Francois Boissevain, was born in 1856 and died in 1929 in Strathmore, Alberta. He was born into a very wealthy family of bankers that took part in financing the development of the Canadian Pacific Railway line. The town of Boissevain in Manitoba is named because of this connection.

Greetings from Canada

This card was mailed by Gerrit Jan Haverkamp on September 23, 1913 from Medicine Hat, Alberta to the widow G. van de Vlekkert in Epe.

We are all healthy.

We saw in the paper the blow that hit you that Leida has passed away. That is very sad for you. We are with you in your suffering.

Many greetings,
G. J. Haverkamp and family

Gerrit Jan Haverkamp came with his wife and four kids in 1910 to Canada. Gerrit farmed at SE1/4 S-35, T-14, R-3, W of 4th. Haverkamp was born September 9, 1883 in Epe and passed away August 1, 1974 in White Rock, BC. His wife, Everdina de Weerd, was born March 13, 1885 in Olst and passed away May 4, 1941 in Langley, BC.

City Hall and Union Bank of Canada, Winnipeg, Man., Canada

This card was mailed from Winnipeg, Manitoba on June 21, 1914 to Miss M. van den Nauwland in Haarlem.

Dear Cousin:

Hereby, I am announcing the birth of our daughter, Elisabeth. Rie and the little one are doing fine.

Many greetings,

R.H. . . .

This card was mailed from Montreal, Quebec on October 25, 1909 to Almelo.

Dear Mien,

I gladly take the opportunity to congratulate Frans on the occasion of his wedding.

Be a nice and loyal friend of my good and dear sister and support her courageously in the difficult beginnings of her household. With that, you have earned your merit and you are competent [to assist her].

May you receive the plenitude of the Grace of God.

Gerard J.M. Melchers

Dear J and N,

Congratulations on the New Year.

Our household has again enlarged with a big boy. Hil and the little one are healthy. Soon more news.

Greetings
Ge & Hil

This card was mailed from Pearce, Alberta in 1911 to Mr. J. van Ham in Eenrum.

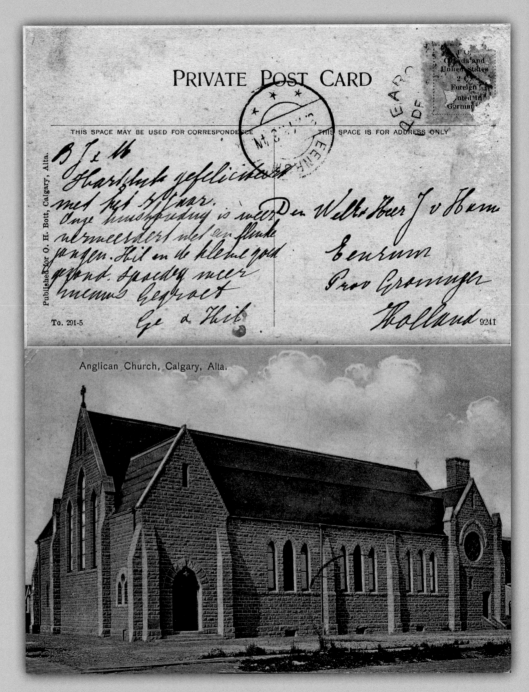

This card was mailed by Kees and Mien Ingwersen from Edmonton, Alberta to Kees' father in Amsterdam on December 18, 1909.

Kees Ingwersen was postmaster in Neerlandia, Alberta from 1925 to 1933.

Dear Parents,
On the 10th of December at 10:30 p.m our well-formed son was born. Happily, everything is all right up to now, however we experienced many difficulties, because I had to manage it nearly all alone without professional help. In about an hour the whole ordeal was over.

You will understand that I am very busy these days. On top of that, I live rather far from the post office and therefore I did not write sooner. For now my best wishes for the coming year. Please inform all of the news since it is impossible to write everyone personally.

With many greetings,
Your loving Son and Daughter
Kees and Mien

Surrounding Area

This card was mailed by Nicolaas van Roon from Oshawa, Ontario on September 3, 1907 to Victoria P. van Roon in Buiksloot.

Nicolaas van Roon, age 20, arrived in Quebec on August 2, 1907 aboard the *Canada*.

Captain Dillon's Bridge, Oshawa.

Dear B and S.
Hereby you are finally receiving a postcard of my city, showing a stream that comes out of the mountains through several waterfalls and a bridge over it. It is clear to see that it is a hilly area here, it is beautiful here.

Affectionately Yours
your son N. v. Roon

From N. van Roon, P.O. Oshawa, Ont., Canada

This card was mailed on January 21, 1909 from Montreal, Quebec to Mr. Leo N. Rientsma in Oegstgeest.

Dear Leo,

A special and lovely card for you.

Likely you have noticed by my picture postcard from Albany, that I have gone to Canada. Everything here is ice and snow, something that is for you. Over the Canadian plains everything white and here by the rocky hills, quite high, a nice view. Montreal is located below. I walk here through the streets, between barricades of snow, 2 to 3 metres wide and 1½ metres high. At Mount Royal they are now busy building an ice palace. With the electric they pickup large pieces, ½ square meter and 3 or 4 decimetres thick out of the St. Lawrence or a lake. Furthermore the weather is mild and it began to thaw.
But that can change quickly here. Yesterday—20 degrees below zero.
Many greetings to everybody,

Saluto, Jacob

Montreal, New Lookout on top of the Mountain

This card was mailed by A. Johan on May 4, 1910 from Toronto, Ontario to Rotterdam.

Via England

Miss,

Receive again three cards of Montreal. The remaining this week. I hope that you like them. Yours faithfully

A. Johan

See here also a waterfall between the mountains.

Greetings from me,

J. van Laan

This card was mailed on March 1, 1906 from a Railway Post Office in British Columbia, to Gilbertus van Hoogervest (1861-1928), who is known to have opened an architecture office in Amsterdam in 1910.

This card was mailed on July 21, 1913 from Windsor, Ontario to Egbert Leegstra in Klazienaveen.

VICTORIA AVE., WINDSOR, CANADA.

Dear Brother,
I am here at this moment. It
is Sunday this evening. I shall
answer your letter.
Your Brother, J.E.

Jan Egbert Sietse Leegstra, a carpenter, was born January 24, 1884 in Veendam. He and his family, his wife Jentje Beuker and their two children Eefke and Jantje, would move to Detroit in 1914.

This card was mailed by Marie Kamstra on June 24, 1911 from Winnipeg, Manitoba to Miss Catharina Wilhelmina Kamstra, in Amsterdam. She was the daughter of Marie Kamstra's brother-in-law, Paulus Kamstra. He was born December 15, 1869 in Franeker and was married to Jolina Wilhelmina van Meerloo, born September 25, 1875 in Amsterdam.

Dear Toos:
How do you like this card? This is September 5 [Labour Day] — then almost everyone goes out. This is the main street, as good as the Kalverstraat in Amsterdam, but this one is much broader. Right away, you see all kinds of things, tram, ambulance, autos, buggies—and all kinds of stuff.

Dear Toos, many kisses from Aunt Marie and Uncle Cor and little [Johanna].

Bye!

Marie's husband, Jan Cornelis Kamstra, was born February 17, 1873 in Franeker. He was a "peddler of vegetables", according to the 1911 Census of Canada. They lived in East Kildonan, Winnipeg amongst other Dutch immigrants, and had one daughter, Johanna, born in 1910. They had arrived in Canada aboard the *Corsican* which docked in Montreal on April 28, 1908. Marie Kamstra died in November of 1942.

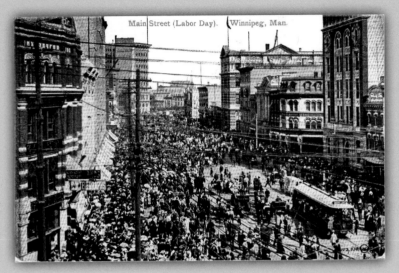

Sunday 6 October 1907

Dear R.,
This card shows a store with six floors.
You can get everything there, food,
clothes and shoes, ironwork, furniture,
all you need. . . there are clerks and
sales ladies.

Greetings from your loving T. van Ark

Post Office Louise Bridge Winnipeg
British N. America

This card was mailed by Timen
van Ark from Winnipeg,
Manitoba on October 7, 1909
to Hendrika R. Lankwarden
in Apeldoorn. She and Timen
were married March 9, 1912 in
Apeldoorn.

Van Ark was born December 2,
1881 in Heerde, and he died in
Apeldoorn December 15, 1938.
Lankwarden was born in 1885
in Apeldoorn and passed away
there on May 5, 1928.

Dear Reverend!
I send a bird's-eye view of my town
and advise about sending the letter
concurrently with this card. In case
this card like many others gets lost,
you know that I did send it, thus you
should have received two from me. I
hope to hear something more in order
to have the cause march on all right.

Many greetings,

Your servant
R.E. de Zwart.

Sent by R. E. de Zwart, Chesley/Ont/Canada Box 173

This card was mailed from Chesley, Ontario by R. E. de Zwart on October 30, 1911 to the Reverend Dr. Willem Jodocus Mathias Engelberts, Amsterdam. Engelberts' 1898 thesis was a biography on Willem Teelinck, a 16th century Dutch minister, which is still available to purchase. Engelberts passed away at age 72 on November 10, 1940 in Hilversum.

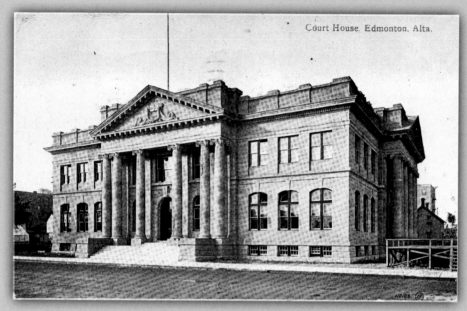

This card was mailed from Edmonton, Alberta January 1915 to Mr. Tj. R. van Gosliga in Greonterp.

Dear Grandfather, Grandmother, and Uncle,

On Sunday we received your letter in good order. This is the Courthouse in Edmonton. When you write us again, tell me which picture postcards you have received then I will not mail to you the same ones again.

Greetings from all of us.

Jelte

POST OFFICE. CPR. EMPRESS HOTEL & INNER HARBOR. VICTORIA B.C.   No. 122.

William Jacobus (Jac) Semeijn (1890–1952) was an important architect in Victoria, B.C. He married Yvette Germaine Cross in Victoria. Some of the buildings in Victoria that Semeyn designed have a heritage designation.

This card was mailed by William Jacobus Semeijn from Victoria, British Columbia on February 18, 1911 to his brother, Harm Semeijn, in Amsterdam.

Dear Brother:

This is a view of the most important part of Victoria. On the foreground now, instead of the rock, there a new steamboat wharf being built. I am healthy and have lots of work at the moment. How are things in Amsterdam? Received now and then a bundle of Prinsen magazines. I almost devour them.

My thanks, Jac.

This card was mailed from L'Isle-aux-Grues, Quebec in August 1911 to Mrs. Annie Kaarssijpesteijn. She was then living on a large country estate, known as *Zuiderhout*, in Heemstede. She belonged to a very wealthy family that owned, among other businesses, the Netherlands Linoleum Factory in Wormerveer.

Dear Aunt,

Here a picture of our island. It is a sweltering 100 degrees in the shade. Therefore I sit most of the time in the water. The ladies here make sugar, which is pressed from trees and that during the enormous heat!

Greetings also for . . .

Your dear nephew, Willem

This card was mailed from Oshawa, Ontario on August 20, 1907 to Hendricus Leonardus Looijestein in Amsterdam. 'Leno', a sailor in the Dutch Navy, was born around 1880 in The Hague. He married Cornelia van der Wal on January 31, 1901 in Den Helder. She was born in Den Helder on June 26, 1876. They had a son Hendricus Leonardus who was born on May 4, 1901 also in Den Helder.

Dear Leno,

I send you a picture of beautiful Canada. Everything is all right. Greetings,

Jo, Mien and Truus.

CARNEGIE PUBLIC LIBRARY, WINNIPEG MAN.

This card was mailed on February 17, 1908 in Headingly, Manitoba to Giessendam.

John Blokland, age 37, arrived October 25, 1907 in Quebec aboard the *Tunisian*.

Dear Friend Walraven,

Here is my new world, where I have been since October 28, 1907. I always had the intention to see something more of the world. It is always the same in Holland. In case I hear from you, I will write more to you soon. Further, many respects for you and many greetings also to the family and to P. F. Terlouw. It is going very well with me. And for me, I live happily.

John Blokland

Headingly near Capt Mat. Mieneke near Winnipeg.

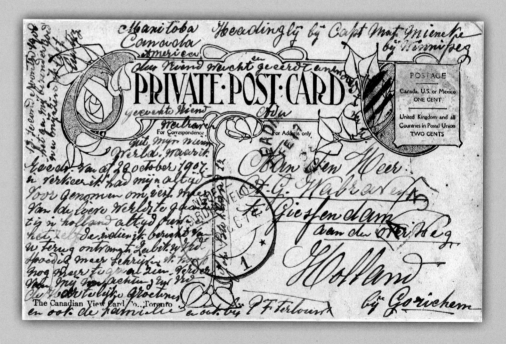

Canadian Harvesting Scenes Reaping

This card was mailed to Mr. Jozeph Meittner from Saskatchewan, arriving in Scheveningen on October 12, 1909.

Joseph and Jeanne,

You asked me for some postcards. Now we can have some of the villages around. When there is the time for me I go to the station. I will think about you.

Your sister, Rosa

Greetings from Canada

This card showing Victoria Bridge was mailed on August 4, 1908 from Hamilton, Ontario to Willem Wils, bookbinder, in Haarlem. Wils was born on April 4, 1870 in Haarlem. He married Hendrika Elisabeth Granneman on May 30, 1895 in Bloemendaal.

Victoria Bridge, Grand Trunk R. R. Depot, Montreal.

Dear Willem:

Well, I should think we don't need to be in Holland to see a very long bridge. How do you like this one? This is the biggest bridge of Canada. I am sleepy now. Good night. Many good wishes for you and your family.

From your brother-in-law,
Jake Groenenberg.

Jacob 'Jake' Groenenberg, a tailor, his wife and three children arrived in Quebec aboard the *Southwark* on May 20, 1907. He was born on April 18, 1876 in Piershil. He married Elisabeth Klazina Schilpzand in Bloemendaal on July 5, 1900. It would appear from other correspondence between Groenenberg and Wils, dated June 1910, that Jake and his family settled later near Canal Dover, Ohio, USA.

One of the many large buildings. Extremely hot here. Because of heat, many dead on the street.

Yours G.

This card was mailed on June 28, 1913 from Toronto, Ontario to Mr. A. H. Vandersteen, tax collector, in Sas van Gent.

C.P.R. Building, Toronto, Canada   Corner King and Yonge Streets,

This card was mailed from Agassiz, British Columbia, August 23, 1910 to Mrs. Reina Hollenga Boon in Zutphen.

This is a well known health resort. It is located on the railway which I travel on almost everyday. In one word it is beautiful. . . .

This is possibly from Daniel Simon Hollenga. He was born September, 23 1878 in Veendam. His father Hans Daniel was born on November 21, 1845 and his mother Reina Boon was born on February 17,1848, both in Veendam.

Hollenga emigrated to the USA and soon after was working for the Seattle Taxicab Company. He worked about one year for the Western division of the CPR emigration department, after which he worked 18 months for Canadian Northern Railroad Company.

He also worked for Western Realty Company in Portage la Prairie in Manitoba until February 15, 1914 when he started working as the secretary of the Chamber of Commerce in Minot, North Dakota. Daniel served as a Colonel in the US army during WWI. Daniel passed away in November 1967, in Lakewood Ocean, New Jersey.

Glacier, B.C., Canadian Rockies

600139

Dear Parents,

Today I have been with two friends to the Niagara waterfall. We were able to profit from cheap train tickets. The impression was overwhelming. I hope to write you soon more about it.
Many greetings,

Johan

The only thing I do not like here is that we have to go further on tomorrow.

Best greetings,
Martin Sieber, Albert Krauze

This card was mailed from Toronto, Ontario on July 5, 1909 to W. Verschoor, a teacher of religion in Nijmegen.

Johan Verschoor was born September 29, 1883 in Lent and was a draftsman. The line following 'Johan' is translated from German and is signed by the two friends accompanying Johan Verschoor referred to in his note.

NIAGARA FALLS in Winter   General View from New Bridge

1116

69

This card was mailed from Niagara Falls, Ontario on June 16, 1908 to Mrs. van Vliet in Haarlem, the widow of K.C. van Vliet-Verfaille.

Dear Madame,

I sit here now looking at the waterfall. For now I am very content and would like to write you a letter, however I can tell you about it much better later on.

Many greetings,

G. Hoekstra

Nineteen-year-old Tjepke van der Weerdt arrived August 2, 1907 in Quebec aboard the *Canada*.

It is quite a nice place. The farm is not big. I am here more for the horses. Therefore I can now learn to handle and steer horses. About cows I know enough now.

Now greetings,
Your loving son T.

My address is . . . c/o Mr. Croley, Box 91, Saltcoats

This card was mailed from Saltcoats, Saskatchewan on February 5, 1910 to Miss Anna van der Weerdt in Leeuwarden, the sister of Tjepke van der Weerdt. Their father, Pieter van de Weerdt, born September 6, 1860 in Sneek, was a butter maker. Their mother was Pietje Kalma born May 27, 1864 in Kampen. A sister, Sjoukje, born June 7, 1891 in Leeuwarden, left Holland on May 17, 1909 for Manitoba.

THE GRIST MILL, Saltcoats, Sask.

City Hall, Montreal

These cards were mailed on November 21, 1909 and February 2, 1911 to Mrs. and Mr. Sollmann in Arnhem. Philippus Sollmann, a merchant, was born in 's-Graveland. He married Anna Cornelia Magdalena Schooleman, on February 3, 1876 in Utingeradeel. Philippus passed away December 26, 1914 in Arnhem.

Richard Sollmann arrived September 7, 1901 in Quebec aboard the *Canada*.

— *cut the letter open on the side*

This is a view of one of the boundaries of the city, a view of the area around the St. James Cathedral (the building with the round dome on top). It is an English Presbyterian church.

Rich

City Hall in winter.

I think I mailed already before a card showing this. This is shown from the side. The fire engines and ambulances and electric reparation cars fly here, normally in the shape of sledges — ling, ling, bang, bang, do you hear the bells? In front of the steam hose are four horses. There are ten fire stations at all parts of the city, the machinery flies with lighting speed out the doors.

This card was mailed by Gerrit Jan Holtrigter from Carlyle, Saskatchewan to Lent on December 12, 1908.

I wish you Salvation and Blessing for the coming Christmas days. The reverse is a partial view of our village. I visited the church with the tower on the corner. If you look further into the card, across the barren land. There is my home, about a ½ hour from the village. It is very cold, little snow.

Many Greetings, G.J. Holtrigter

Holtrigter came to Canada in 1893 aboard the *Numidian* with the first organized group of Dutch immigrants to Winnipeg. He became a successful farmer. He would marry Geraldina Wesselina Rondeel in 1913 in Carlyle. In 1926, they returned to Holland and lived in Apeldoorn to his death in 1937.

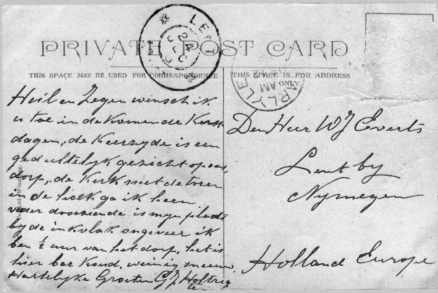

73

Field and River from Lower Trail, B.C.

This card was mailed from Fort MacLeod, Alberta to Willem Wallegien in Dedemsvaart July, 17, 1908.

Wallegien was born September 27, 1868 in Avereest, and passed away there on December 1, 1948.

Hereby a few prints of this wonderland for your boys. I haven't had the time to write, but be patient because when it comes, perhaps it will be too much to cope with.

Greetings, s'il vous plaît, to all our acquaintances and especially to you and your family.

J.G.T.

Jan George Tersteeg, born in 1878, married Jenneken Steenbergen on July 14, 1904 in Avereest. She was born September 19, 1871 in Avereest. In 1907, Tersteeg purchased a quarter section near Pearce, Alberta.

6
Messages

This card was mailed from Raymore, Saskatchewan on March 1, 1909 to Zoeterwoude. Due to the lack of a cancel stamp with a location and date, the local postmaster handwrote the date of cancel.

Many greetings from your brother.

J. Schipper
Charlottenhof
Sask., Canada

Jacob Schipper, born in 1876, came to Canada in 1902. He farmed at NE 1/4, S-24, T-28, R-18, W of 2nd. According to the census of 1911, Schipper lived with two domestic aids, William Duncan of Scotland, age 23, and Arend van der Knaap of Holland, also age 23.

This card was mailed by Jozeph Bank on June 12, 1909 from Winnipeg, Manitoba to his sister in Ijmuiden, Adriana Margaretha Maria Antonia, born September 16, 1886 in Den Helder.

Dear Sister,

I first thought for a moment to mail you quickly a picture postcard and to inform you that I am doing fine. It is beautiful weather the last weeks and quite warm. How is your eye? Did you already buy a lorgnet or not? I hope everything will be all right, however take good care of yourself. Many greetings to Mother and father and the boys .

As always your loving brother Jozeph
Excuse my writing, the pen is very bad.

Jozeph Petrus Bernardus Antonius Bank was born October 13, 1884 in Den Helder. He was removed from the IJmuiden Municipal Record on January 15, 1907 with the comment that he was to go to Canada. IJmuiden is the place where his father was a fish merchant.

Best Wishes and Regards from the far west.

from G. W. Bruggencate

This card was written to J. Prakken, head of the school in Enter, Overijssel. It was mailed from Prince Albert, Saskatchewan on August 31, 1908, arriving in Enter on September 12, 1908.

The writer is Gerhardus Warnerus 'Charles or Chas.' ten Bruggencate (b. 1873), an accountant and cigar trader from Utrecht. According to Saskatchewan homestead records, he had received a quarter section of land at Steep Creek in the Prince Albert area. He was murdered on or about February 12, 1913, near Prince Albert. *The Sessional Papers of the Dominion of Canada 1914*, report that the murder occurred after a drunken encounter at the cabin of Louis Racz and Emeri Kovach. Bruggencate was well-known in town, and especially well-known to police, having served terms in the local jail, himself. He died after receiving a fractured skull and cut throat at the hands of Racz and Kovach. They were arrested on vagrancy, but once in custody, one accused the other. After the first trial both were sentenced to death, which was later commuted to life imprisonment following other trials in which they continued to accuse each other of the crime.

The records of the administration of 1921 show that 'Chas.' ten Bruggencate's estate went to his widow, Christina Szopko, who had remarried sometime after his death. His brother, Hendrik Jan ten Bruggencate (b. April 29, 1875), had arrived in Halifax, N.S. on March 23, 1907. According to the 1916 census, Hendrik lived in North Battleford, Saskatchewan.

8th Avenue, Calgary, Alta.

This card was mailed on February 25, 1912 from Calgary, Alberta to Amerongen.

Many greetings to all of you from your friend,

T. Ploeg

221–10th St., Hillhurst, Calgary, Alberta, Canada

Teunis Ploeg was born February 12, 1892 in Amerongen. He arrived as a 19 year old in New York on April 25, 1911.

C. P. R. Engineering Department
Strathmore, Alta.

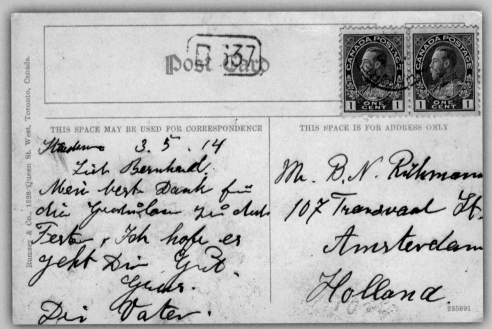

This card was mailed by Marcus Rühmann on May 3, 1914 from Strathmore, Alberta to his son, Bernard Nicolaas Rühmann, in Amsterdam.

Strathmore 3. 5. 14

Dear Bernhard,

My thanks for the momento you also celebrate. I hope that you are doing fine.

Greetings,

Your Father

Marcus Rühmann was born on April 26, 1863 in Ebendorf, Germany. He married Anna Elisabeth Freund who was born February 22, 1867 in Amsterdam. Rühmann was described in the 1889 Amsterdam Municipal Register as a shopkeeper. He left for Canada in 1913 as a 'workman'.

This card was mailed on February 7, 1911 from Toronto, Ontario to G. M. van Middelkoop in Alkmaar.

According to the newspaper *Het Nieuws van den Dag*, Miss van Middelkoop was appointed as a teacher in a temporary position in Alkmaar on February 2, 1912.

The best wishes for your next exams.

Elly

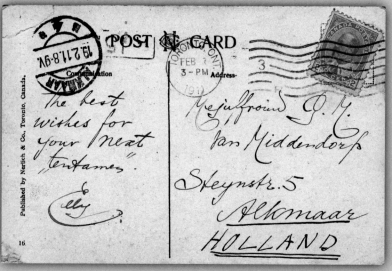

This card was mailed to
Miss Betsie Straub on
September 25, 1909 from
Quebec to Amsterdam.

Best greetings

from Willem

Avenue Road & St Pauls Methodist Church
Toronto Canada

This card was mailed by Ferdinand Maximiliaan Broekman on July 8, 1911 from Toronto, Ontario to Groningen.

Dear Truus!

Many greetings also to Uncle and Aunt
from Ferdinand

693 Richmond Ave. W.
Toronto. Ont., Canada

Broekman was born February 12, 1891 in Groningen.

This card was mailed from Alberta in 1911 to R. Ubels in Arnhem.

Ubels was a druggist who had arrived in Arnhem on March 20, 1905 from Baarn and would leave there on February 3, 1912 for Amersfoort.

Greetings from Evert

Buffalo Lake, near Stettler, Alberta.

PRIVATE POST CARD

Published by W. J. Hart, Alberta Drug Co., Stettler, Alberta.

THIS SPACE MAY BE USED FOR CORRESPONDENCE

THIS SPACE IS FOR ADDRESS ONLY

Gegroet van.

Evert

Den Wel Edele Heer.
R. Ubels.
Hommelscheweg
Holland
Arnhem

Greetings from Canada

This card was most likely mailed by August 'Guus' Meijer from Winnipeg, Manitoba to Cornelia Otter, in Utrecht on October 28,1907. Cornelia (also a Meijer from another family) married Cornelis Otter on June 28, 1893 in Utrecht. Cornelis Otter is the brother of Guus' wife, Antonetta Otter.

August Julius Meijer married Antonetta Jacoba Otter on August 9,1899 in Utrecht. According to the 1911 census, Meijer (also spelled Meyer) arrived in Canada in 1907, followed by his wife 'Anna' and their two children in 1908.

My dear sister, Cornelia,

I send to you my greetings from this country and hope you are living good with my . . . My wife is expecting a child, but you cannot tell.

For the second time, my greetings, Your Brother, Guus

This card was mailed by Anna Geel in Winnipeg, Manitoba to the family Schaefer (former neighbours) in Hilversum on November 11, 1907, then forwarded to Bussem.

Anna Geel is the sister of Dieuwertje Geel, who was married to Anthonius Cornelis Wouters. She would marry Siepko Voorsmit on October 25, 1910 in Winnipeg, Manitoba.

Address, A.C. Wouters

Post Box 86, Winnipeg, Man.

Dear Friends,

I do not know which postcards I mailed you. Perhaps Mister Schaefer has this card already. We are still doing fine here and hope you are, too. Many greetings from my sister and her husband and Corry and me.

Anna Geel

Dear Family,

I hope you receive this card in good health. I hope to receive good news very soon and a thousand kisses, Mother.

Say hello to everybody,

Salomon and Maurits

MONTREAL.—St. James Methodist Church.

This card was mailed to Miss Frederica Cohen on January 11, 1905 from Montreal to Amsterdam.

Toronto from Parliament Buildings

This card was mailed on October 24, 1910 by Frans Palfenier from Acton, Ontario to Miss Maria Magdalena Neumeier in Amsterdam. Maria was born on January 1, 1889 in Amsterdam and was removed from the Amsterdam Municipal Register on May 7, 1913. Canadian records show that she married Frans in Winnipeg, Manitoba on May 30, 1913, according to the *Acton Free Press*, June 5, 1913.

Yours,
F. Palfenier

Toronto, October 17, 1910

Frans Palfenier was born on October 4, 1887 in Amsterdam where he was registered as an office clerk. He was removed from the Amsterdam Municipal Register on December 13, 1909, with the comment that he was to go to Canada.

KAKABEKA FALLS   NEAR FORT WILLIAM, ONT

This card was mailed from Fort Williams, Ontario on September 22, 1907 to Heinrich Wilhelm Schäperkotter in Amsterdam. Schäperkotter was born April 14, 1857 in Amsterdam. He bottled beer for a living.

Greetings

T. Grimme

This card was mailed from
Montreal by K. Dral on
October 31, 1905 to his brother
Jan Gerrits Dral in Grouw,
Friesland. Jan Gerrits was born
November 23, 1865 in
Venhuizen and at the time of this
card was the chief machinist at
the local water works in Grouw.

"Corsican", in the Lachine Rapids.

No. 919 Published by The Montreal News Company, Montreal-Leipzig-Berlin

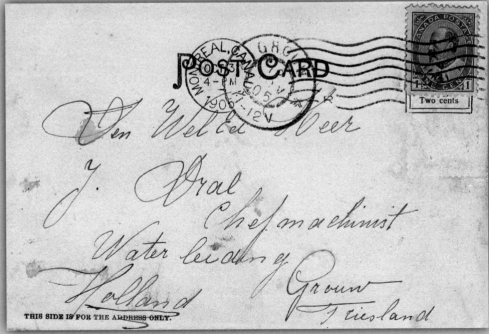

Many greetings from Canada.

Your Brother
K. Dral

This card was mailed by J. Eggerdink on March 14, 1911 from Winnipeg, Manitoba to Hilversum.

A.A.J. Kleuters

Many greetings and wishes from

J. Eggerdink
13 March 1911

St. Mary's Catholic Church, Winnipeg, Man.

This card was mailed to B. Pfaltzer from Toronto, Ontario on July 31, 1899 to Amsterdam. Pfaltzer owned a wholesale firm dealing in watches and clocks.

Many Greetings from Toronto, from your

P. Laudenberger

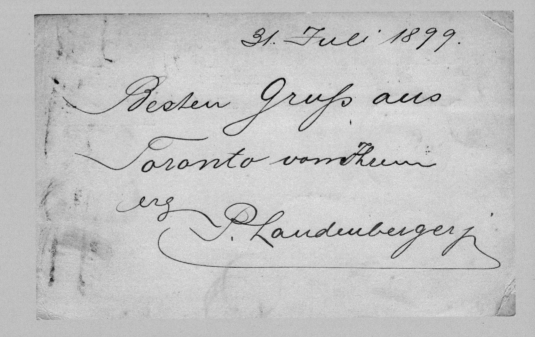

Main Street, looking North, Winnipeg, Man., Canada

This card was mailed by Jan Halbes de Boer from Winnipeg on November 24, 1913 to A. de Jong in Dronrijp.

Dear Niece and Nephew:

Hereby I am letting you know that my address is not the same and don't write to me before I send you a new address. The letters that are on their way will still come into my possession.

Greetings from Jan de Boer.

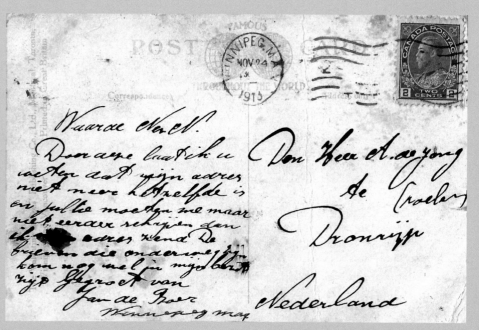

Jan Halbes de Boer was born on July 26, 1887 in Friesland. He worked as a railway worker and left the Dronrijp area for Winnipeg on April 9, 1912.

Dear Friends,

Receive this in health. Say "Hello" to our acquaintances. If you are to make a little trip this summer, perhaps you will also stop here with us.

To all of you, many greetings from us.

H. Esveld

386 Jasper Avenue, Winnipeg Canada (Man.)

Esveld, born December 8, 1886, left Amsterdam with his wife Adriane and daughter Annie for Winnipeg in 1906. He married Adriane on April 10, 1906 in Amsterdam. He passed away in Winnipeg on November 22, 1918 after contracting the Spanish Flu.

This card was sent by Hendrik Esveld on August 8, 1910 from Winnipeg, Manitoba to Johannes Frederik Muller (b. 1857) who ran a flower shop in Amsterdam.

POST CARD

CORRESPONDENCE HERE | NAME AND ADDRESS HERE

Kenora June 21st '13
Hartelyk gegr.
Br. zw.
Herman

J. v. Breevoort J. Esq
Bloemgracht 15
Amsterdam.
(Holland)

Kenora June 21, '13
Many greetings.

Brother and Brother-in-law
Herman

This card was mailed to J. van Breevoort from Kenora, Ontario on June 21, 1913 to Amsterdam.

Hello

This card was mailed from Winnipeg by Nicolaas Jilles Cornelis van Geelen, on March 17, 1913, to Pieter Jacobus van Geelen. Pieter was a silversmith, born October 14, 1874 in Schoonhoven.

This card was mailed from Seely's Bay, Ontario to Mathilda Akerboom in Amsterdam in May of 1911.

This card was mailed on April 11, 1914 from Winnipeg to W. Mantel in Andijk.

The card was mailed by Coba from Montreal, Quebec to Miss J. van Galen in Loosduinen on May 20, 1907.

This card was mailed in July of 1913 to 's-Gravenhage (The Hague) from Montreal, Quebec. The author is likely Josephus Antonius Verbruggen, a furniture maker born February 6, 1878 in Den Bosch. He married Henrica Geertruida Vogel on November 24, 1900 in Den Bosch. He left for London from The Hague with his family on March 12, 1907. According to the United Stated Federal Census, by 1930, he is listed as living in Hennepin, Minnesota.

This card was mailed on August 13, 1910 by Theodorus Petrus van Velzen (b. August 6, 1889 in Zoeterwoude) from Winona, Ontario to his sister Barbara Adriana van Velzen in Leiden. She was born April 20,1894 in Zoeterwoude and would become a teacher. On October 29, 1934 in Leiden, she married Willem Antonie Bergers (b. October 20, 1895 in Leiden).

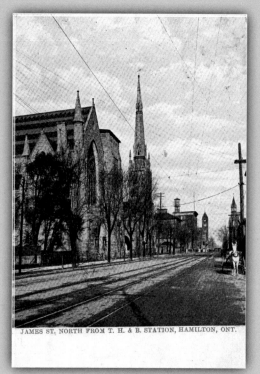

JAMES ST, NORTH FROM T. H. & B. STATION, HAMILTON, ONT.

This card was mailed by Jacobus Cornelis Smal from Toronto on April 2, 1913 to J. D. van der Einden, a mailman in Haarlem. Smal worked as a plasterer and was born on February 27, 1888 in Haarlem. Smal married Gerarda Fronsisca de Grant on May 15, 1912 in Amsterdam. The records show that he was removed from the Haarlem Municipal Register on March 17, 1913, with the comment that he was leaving for Toronto.

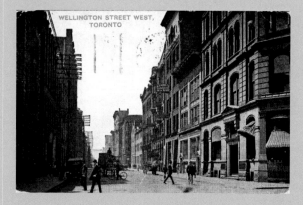

WELLINGTON STREET WEST, TORONTO

This card was mailed by P. Roukema on June 22, 1912 from Toronto, Ontario to Anne Roukema in Leeuwarden. Anne Roukema was born March 18, 1859 in Lemmer and was married to Geertje de With, who was born May 7, 1851 in Oosterzee. Anne Roukema was proprietor of the Oranje Bierhuis, to this day the most authentic café in Leeuwarden.

This card was mailed on October 5, 1913 by E. Anceaux, (b. May 11, 1888 in Rotterdam) from Halifax, Nova Scotia to Rotterdam.

St. John's Park, Winnipeg, Man.

This card was mailed to the family of Hendrik Johannes Mink, by Johannes Nicolaas Dumans from Winnipeg to Utrecht on May 10, 1912. Mink was a stained glass artist. He was married to Bardina Kastelijn.

Johannes Nicolaas Dumans, a typesetter, was born September 17, 1886 in Utrecht. He left for Canada on April 3, 1912. The records show that he made three trips back to The Netherlands between 1916 and 1925.

This card was mailed from Winnipeg on February 25, 1915 to Mr. Francois Dellaert in Sas Van Gent.

Gerrit Swier (b. 1888/1889 in Enkhuizen) mailed this card from Prince Albert to Zaandam on May 15, 1913. On April 20, 1916, he married Aagje Beumer (b. July 22, 1888 in Zaandam).

High Level Bridge, Edmonton, Alta.

This card was mailed from Edmonton, Alberta on July 11, 1914 to W. Mantel, likely from Jan Mantel, who came to Canada in 1907 with his wife Ytze and three children.

This card was mailed by Emma van Dijk on March 9, 1912 from Edmonton, Alberta to Miss A. Aperloo in Genemuiden.

Jasper Avenue, Edmonton, Alta.

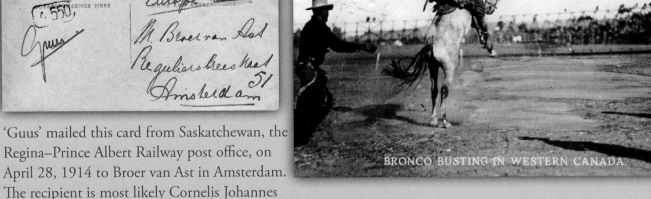

BRONCO BUSTING IN WESTERN CANADA.

'Guus' mailed this card from Saskatchewan, the Regina–Prince Albert Railway post office, on April 28, 1914 to Broer van Ast in Amsterdam. The recipient is most likely Cornelis Johannes van Ast, born November 25, 1871 in Rotterdam. His profession is listed in the Amsterdam Municipal Register as a restaurant owner.

This card was mailed by Johannes E. Hueting on August 5, 1912 from Calgary to Sergeant G. J. Voigt in Kampen. Voigt would pass his exams to become an infantry officer on August 21, 1912. On April 12, 1919, Voigt married M. Brouwer in Batavia, Dutch East Indies.

8th Avenue, Calgary, Alta.

Hueting, his wife and three children (Ada, Margrette and Johannes) would eventually move from Calgary to Noyes, Minnesota.

Main St. North. Winnipeg, Man.

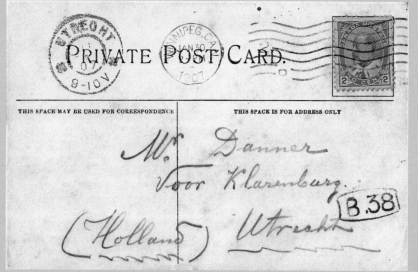

This card was sent by W. Eggink from Winnipeg, Manitoba on January 30, 1907, to W. Danner in Utrecht. W. Danner is likely related to F.H. Danner, a book binder in Utrecht, still in business today.

Greetings from Winnipeg,

W. Eggink

New Year's Wishes

WINDSOR STATION. C. P. RAILWAY. MONTREAL.

Dear Brother Leo,

We hope that you are still healthy, which is the case for both of us. This week we received your postcards in the best condition and noticed that you are still doing all right. I can also inform you that I have a document from the Consul that says the following: that the next conscription to which I belong will not be summoned, but if I want to go at my own cost, I can safely do that, but I have no time.

Receive furthermore many greetings from your brother and sister Mauris and Siska with the best wishes from 1915.
Goodbye.

This card was mailed by Mauris van Geel on December 18, 1914 from Montreal, Quebec to Bangsal-Modjokerto, Java, Dutch East Indies.

This card was mailed from Montreal, Quebec on December 28, 1913 to Bertha Margaretha Broeckhuijsen in The Hague. Broeckhuijsen was born on February 17, 1892 in The Hague.

The writers are probably Gerardus Josephus 'Jo' and Petrus Johannes 'Jan' Nijbacker, sons of Hendrikus Nijbacker and Gerarda Elisabeth Niessen. Jan was born on May 4, 1892 and Jo was born on March 12, 1894.

Many hearty wishes for 1914.

Jo and Jan Nijbacker

Greetings from Canada

This card was mailed by F. Lotgering on December 2, 1909 from Montreal, Quebec to J.G. Opbroek in Haarlem.

Opbroek was a lead and zinc worker, as well as gas and water fitter with a later address, Generaal Cronjestraat 74, Haarlem.

Dear Friends:

Hello. How are you? Everyone all right? I hope so. My best wishes for the year '10.

From your friend,

F. Lotgering

p.s. Kiss my wife for me, please.

Dear Ham and friends,

With pleasure I received your card and I do thank you for the New Year's wish and I also wish you all a happy and prosperous New Year. I thought that I had already been forgotten by you, since I did not hear anything from the old acquaintances and learn now that you all doing fine. With us, things go the way that I had already written about to Mister Karres as he probably has told you. We are fortunately healthy and have no financial complaints. In the coming spring I hope to move to Montreal. Dear Ham and all friends, many greeting from your always loving,

A.C. Ros

This card was mailed by Antonius Christianus Ros on January 19, 1909 at Berthier-en-Haut, Quebec to Amsterdam, addressed to Hendrik Jan Toekamp Lammers, a merchant in wines and distilled liquors.

Anthonius Christianus Ros (b. March 23, 1873, Amsterdam) and his wife, Anna Maria Wilhelmina Waagemans (b. July 10, 1873, Amsterdam). Ros, an office clerk, with his wife and three children departed on November 23, 1911 from Amsterdam for Montreal.

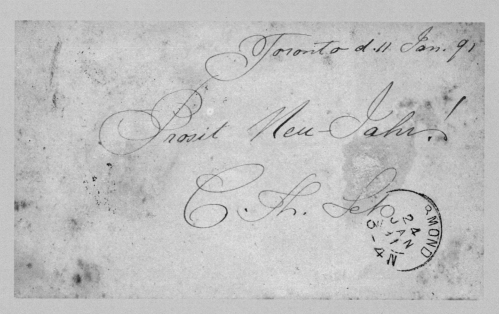

Salute to the New Year!   C. Th. S . . .

The card was mailed on January 12, 1891 from Toronto, Ontario to L.G.E. Gertsen, LL.M., a clerk of the court in Roermond.

This card was mailed on December 22, 1894 from Toronto, Ontario to Romkje Kuipers in Utrecht. Romkje Kuipers was born June 17, 1871 in Sneek. She married Alexander Petrus van der Kruk, on May 24, 1899 in Utrecht.

Dear Romkje,

You have to share the same fortune with Anna and Cato by being content with this card.

Much salvation and blessing with the commencement of the New Year. I shall write to you soon. On such a card one can write so little. Things are going very well with me.

Greetings from your loving Brother.

Greetings from Canada

Regina Fire Department.

This card was mailed by S. de Vries, on December 20, 1912 from Sleeman, Ontario to Amsterdam.

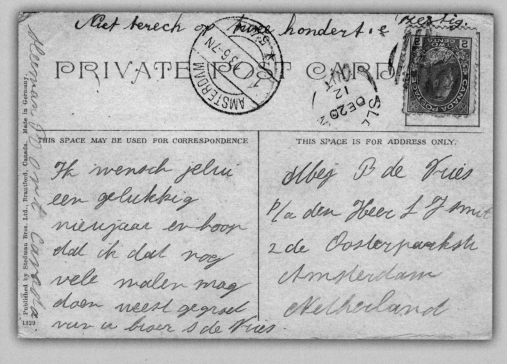

I wish you a happy New Year and hope that I can wish the same many more times.

Many Greetings, from your brother,

S. de Vries

New Post Office on Portage Avenue.

This card was mailed on December 21, 1906 from Winnipeg, Manitoba to Cornelis Herrewijn, a teacher in Willemstad.

Dear Jw. and J.

Toast to your health in the New Year.

Your loving Brother, Jan H.

This card was mailed from Dominion City, Manitoba, to G.W. Van Sante at Hoogvliet by Rotterdam on December 20, 1907.

Dear Friends and family members,

We wish you all a blessed New Year. We are healthy and hope to hear that from you, also.

Amiable greetings,
D. Kap and T. Kap–Van Gelderen

Dirk Kap and Trijntje Kap–Van Gelderen came to Canada in 1905. Dirk Kap was born August 21, 1861 in Oudenhorn. He married Trijntje Van Gelderen, born August 15, 1860 in Spijkenisse. They married on December 3, 1884 in Spijkenisse and farmed near the village of Dominion City, Manitoba. In 1923, they left for St. Louis, Missouri, USA.

The card was sent by Jo Kriekmans on December 19, 1912 from Winnipeg, Manitoba to The Hague.

Dear Family Knook,

At the commencement of this New Year,
I wish you much salvation and blessing.

Jo Kriekmans

p.s. Leendert, thanks for your picture.

C.P.R. DEPOT   WINNIPEG, MAN.

NOVELTY SOUVENIR CO. 614-616 MAIN STREET, WINNIPEG. 1872

This card was mailed by Johannes Cornelissen on January 4, 1908 from Winnipeg, Manitoba to his brother W. Arnold Cornelissen Jr., a medical doctor, and his sister Maria in Deventer.

Cornelissen, age 28, came to Canada in 1907 via New York. In the 1911 Canadian census, he was listed as a "labourer" in the Souris area of Manitoba.

Dear Wil and Maria:

Many good wishes for the New Year—letter follows. I have had no time, yet. I met a colleague of yours, Wil! Everything is OK. Perhaps I will get to a farm in the beginning of June; good conditions. Take care of yourselves,

with a handshake (a paw),
Your Brother, John

Address,
J Cornelissen, Manor Hotel, Winnipeg

ROYAL ALEXANDRA HOTEL, WINNIPEG.

This card was mailed from Winnipeg, Manitoba to Baarn on December 28, 1907 by Willem Zilvestor Schaap to his brother Pieter Dirk Schaap. Pieter Schaap was a carpenter, who was born September 22, 1856 in Eemnes. Willem Zilvestor Schaap was born October 28, 1864 in Baarn.

Dear Brother, Sister and children,

At the commencement of the year 1908, we wish you all much luck and many blessings. We are all still well, and however, it is, at the moment, a slack economy and many are without work. I have, thank God, continuous work to do. A large family needs a lot. I hope that you may receive this in good circumstances and in health. You see, I will never forget you, I can't, and we do not forget again to wish you many greetings,

Your loving brother
W. Z. Schaap

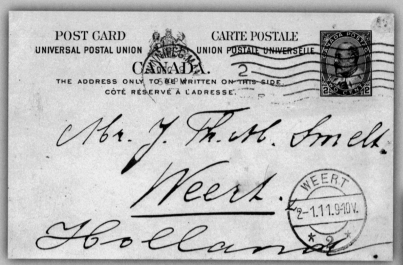

This card was mailed December 19, 1910 from Winnipeg, Manitoba by Jacques M. C. Smelt to his brother and sister-in-law in Weert.

Monday afternoon at 1:20. 19 dec. 1910

Dear Jan and Fien:

Hereby, I send you, as a small present, a newspaper from Montreal, of which I had a subscription from when I was still in Montreal. In all likelihood, I will go further northwards in the beginning of January. I will send you the particulars in a letter.

Much salvation and blessings in 1911.
Yours truly, J. M. C. Smelt

Post Office Winnipeg

With many good wishes for 1911.

Calgary 15 Dec. '10

This card was mailed on December 17, 1910, likely from Calgary, Alberta, to Miss Betting in The Hague.

Canadian Harvesting Scenes : Threshing Wheat

1910

A Merry Christmas from your brother Walter and also for William G.

This card was mailed by Walter Van Dam on December 9, 1910 from Lethbridge, Alberta to The Hague.

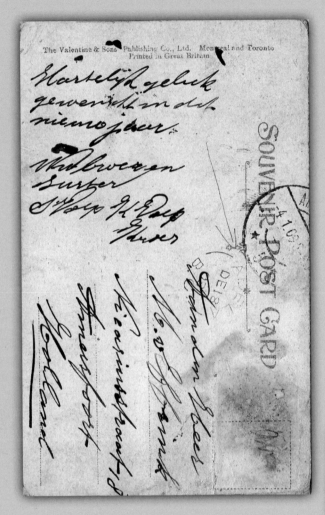

This card was mailed from Adela, British Columbia, to Amersfoort by Steven Volp on December 18, 1908, to Martinus Van Effrink. Van Effrink was married on November 16, 1904, in Amersfoort to Hendrika Maria Volp, sister of Steven Volp.

Effrink was an iron-woker at Hollandsche IJzeren Spoorweg Maatschappij (Dutch Iron Railway Co.).

Steven Volp, born 1871 in Amersfoort, was married in 1897 to Kruintje Kroes, born 1874 in Nijkerk.

Many good wishes for the New Year,

Your Brother and Sister,

Steven Volp and Kruintje Volp-Kroes

This card was mailed from Armstrong, British Columbia to Breda on December 12, 1909 by Arthur and Johannes Cools to their brother-in-law Johannes H. Siepker and his wife, Ludovica J.M. Siepker-Cools.

Dear Jo and Louise,

From the far west we wish you and the family a sainted and happy New Year. That 1910 may be marked by prosperity and health, and that you all will be spared of sickness, misfortune and accidents, is the heartfelt wish of your brothers,

Arthur and Jan

Arthur Martinus Maria Cools was born November 12, 1862 in Tilburg. His brother, Johannes Baptiste Cools was born May 18, 1868 in Tilburg. Arthur worked for the Algemeene Bredaasch Assuarantie-kantoor on the Tuinstraat in Tilburg in 1904. According to the *Nieuwe Tilburgsche Courant* of July 7, 1904, he was selling a building lot and four houses. In 1908, the brothers left for Canada and returned to Tilburg, in 1914. Arthur passed away unmarried on October 17, 1945 in Udenhout.

9

Birthdays

Harvesting Company's Works, Hamilton, Canada

This card was mailed by Johanna Tegelaar-Koch on May 27, 1912, from Hamilton to Eduard Christiaan Pieter Nicola in Amsterdam. Nicola was married to Johanna Geertruida Tegelaar, born August 24, 1882, in Lekkerkerk.

Dear Ed,

Congratulations on your birthday, also from Hendrik and the Bob.

We do not know where you are, however, with crossed-fingers, we sent it to Amsterdam. Also from Jo and Mache, congratulations for the 10th of June. It is too bad that you sold everything. We still feel sorry about selling. Household goods here are expensive and of bad quality, for sure, 3 times more expensive than in Holland.

Many greetings also for Father and Mother from the three of us.
Jo

Johanna 'Jo' Koch was born on August 20, 1880 in Rotterdam. She married Hendrik Tegelaar who was born on May 13, 1879 in Rotterdam. "The Bob" mentioned in the card is their son, Hendrik, born on December 12, 1908. Tegelaar Sr., a machinist, died on November 19, 1928 in York, Ontario.

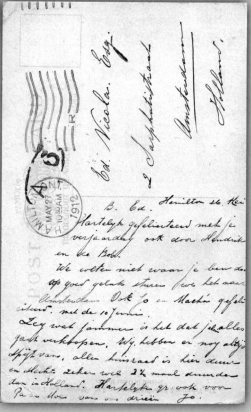

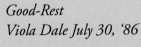

Good-Rest
Viola Dale July 30, '86

My good wishes for August 23. I hope that this postcard arrives in time, according to my calculations a few days too early, but that is better than if it would arrive too late. My husband and I are doing very well. The new country suits me well, only it is very warm. Last year, when we were all together for your birthday in March, I did not think to be so far away now.

With many greetings, also for Abraham
Georgette Money

This card was mailed from Griswold Station, Manitoba, on July 31, 1886 to Carel Willem Alexander Wildeman in Den Haag. Wildeman, born August 8, 1818 in Den Haag, was a retired Major.

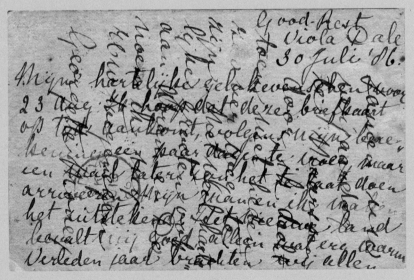

Georgette Melville Gertrude Capadose was born August 29, 1860 in The Hague. She was married on May 10, 1886 in Winnipeg, Manitoba to Sidney Wels Money, born September 26, 1858 in Brighton, Surrey. Her father was Isaak Capadose, who became Coadjutor of the Apostles, in Albury, England in 1876.

Dear Gerdie,
Sincerest congratulations on your birthday and I am sorry that I am not there but that will happen one time. Congratulate for me Father, Mother and Tinny, I will write you soon a letter. Gerdie, again,

With many kisses your loving Nellie!

This card was mailed from Earlie, Alberta, on November 10, 1911 to Gerritdina (Gerdie) Rolina Christina Louise Bunschoten in Utrecht. Bunschoten was born November 27, 1901 in Utrect. Her father was Dirk Jan Bunschoten, a merchant, born in Utrecht on January 18, 1875 and died in Zeist on May 7, 1929.

Bow River and Massive Range, Banff, Alta.

Langdon 2 Nov., 1913

Dear Cousin Jan,
From all of us congratulations on your birthday and since we did not send a picture postcard you will get two. This is view of the Canadian Mountains. A few weeks ago they went to this place to see the Van de Velde's and it supposed to be very beautiful there.

Many greetings, your Aunt Jantje.

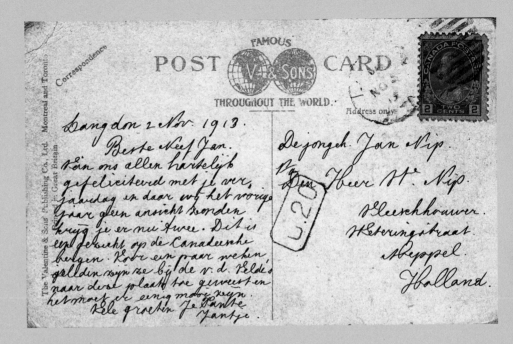

This card was mailed on November 2, 1913 from Langdon, Alberta to Meppel to Jan Nip, c/o Mr. Wiecher Nip, butcher (1871–1960).

Sawback Mount from Hot Springs Road, Banff, Canadian Rockies

Dear Lutske,

We want to congratulate all of you with your birthday. It will be a month too late for sure, however, it is sincere. Our Jo's birthday is tomorrow and she becomes 6 years old. She is already learning quite some English and the little one L., no less. Now dear L., we had enjoyable Christmas days. We even had a nicely decorated Christmas tree in the house. Several children from our neighbours had hung a present in the tree for each of us. Those children sang in front of the tree, also. Our L., it was a delight. Now L., all of us doing fine in the hope to hear from you again.

*Now many greetings from us all
Uncle Aunt and Cousins.*

This card was mailed on January 27, 1913 from Winnipeg, Manitoba to Miss Lutske de Jong in Heerenveen.

This card was mailed on June 4, 1910 from Winnipeg, Manitoba to Willem Jacob Gerlagh in Amsterdam. Gerlagh was born July 9, 1874 and worked as a machinist. He married Wilhelmina Teders on November 10, 1898 in Amsterdam.

Dear N. and N.

Our congratulations on your 14th of June.
J. and M.

Winnipeg, June 8, 1910
417 Andrews Street

This card was mailed by Alphonse Caspar Marie Muskeyn on January 9, 1912 from Raymore, Saskatchewan to J.K. Hensen in Montfoort, head of the public school.

Willem de Gelder, a fellow immigrant was also from Montfoort, arriving in Canada in 1910. His letters are the subject of book entitled A Dutch Homesteader on the Prairies.

Harvest Scene, Canada's Western Prairies.

Dear [School] Master,

Many thanks for the felicitations, so pleasant for me. I coincidentally like the felicitations from the highly respected family de Gelder (also from Willem) received on January 1. It was most pleasant to hear about the promotions of both your sons. Many congratulations with that. The notary informs you continually about my adventures here. Thus you know everything about that. Until now, I have luckily nothing to complain about. All the best for you and your family. Many greetings to all (also uncle John and daughter) and also for you by receiving a hand-shake.

As always, from your affectionate friend, Muskeyn.

You have to keep going here. During the day it is 40 degrees below 0, Fahrenheit.

Muskeyn had been the mayor of IJsselstein and later became mayor of Montfoort en Willeskop, between (1906–1909). He arrived in Quebec on June 4, 1910 aboard the *Laurentic*. In 1911, Muskeyn moved near Oyen, Alberta, where he obtained a quarter section homestead for ranching (SW 1/4 S-13, T-24, R13, W of 4th). He married Theodora Ledon and would later move to Vancouver, where he operated a popcorn franchise in Stanley Park. Muskeyn passed away on November 29, 1960 in Vancouver and is buried at Moutain View Cemetery. His descendants live in the greater Vancouver area.

A Scene in Rockwood Park, St. John N.B.

This card was mailed from Moncton, New Brunswick to Mrs. U. van Elst in Maastricht, on March 15, 1913.

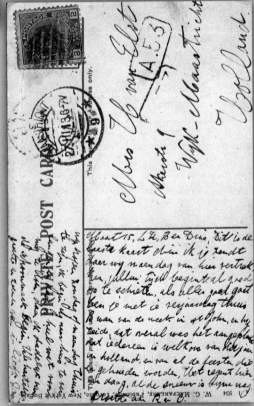

Dear U., B., and Dina,

This is the last card I will send to you because we are leaving here on Monday. Your time starts already to get on, if everything goes well, you will be home on your birthday. B. was in St. John this week and he told us that it was planted everywhere and that everyone is welcome this year in Holland with all the festivities that are being held. It is raining here today, all the snow almost gone. We hope to be home on Sunday or Monday, I begin to long for home and a lot is waiting there for me to do. I start directly with cleaning up.

Many greetings and kisses from your affectionate, Jan

Greetings to R and C.

C.P.R. Station, Fort William, Ont., Canada

This card was mailed to F. ten Hagen on April 22, 1915 from Fort William, Ontario to Weesp.

Dear Cousin,

With this card we congratulate you on your birthday and we hope that you can celebrate that day for many years in health in the presence of Father and Mother. And we wish you further a pleasant day.

Many kisses from your loving cousins, Klaasje and Hendrik Klomp

Main Street, Winnipeg, Man.

This card was mailed on March 26, 1912 from Winnipeg, Manitoba to Miss A. Feenstra in Rotterdam. The address in Rotterdam is in care of K. Feenstra at the Steam Dairy Factory Aurora at the Oostzeedijk in Rotterdam. K. Feenstra was the manager of the factory.

Winnipeg

Dear Auntie:
How are you. I am go to school I have one page for homework. I wish you a very nice birthday.

Louisa Feenstra

General Hospital, Winnipeg, Man.

Dear Toos,

Congratulations on your birthday, and also for Papa and Mama and the little sisters and little brother from Aunt Marie and Uncle Cor. How nicely you and also Zus can already write. Say hello especially to Opoe, Papa, Mama, Aunt Clara, Uncle Van Paassen, and to yourself and the sisters and brother.

Many kisses from Uncle Cor and Aunt Marie

This card was mailed from Winnipeg, Manitoba to Cato Kamstra in Amsterdam February 1911.

Dear Miss Maria,

Again, my well-intentioned congratulations on the remembrance of July 19. There is, for sure, no snow in Breukelen, otherwise I would come on July 19 with the sledge and four dogs to Hoogerlust. Then you and the other ladies could make a sledge journey.

Many pleasures.

Greetings to all s.v.p. from your . . .

Husky Dog Team, Edmonton, Alberta

This card was mailed from Langenburg, Saskatchewan on July 5, 1910 to Maria Verbiest in Breukelen. Verbiest lived on a country estate, Huize Hoogerlust, that was owned by Bernard Verbiest. She married Cor Samson on June 9, 1914 in Breukelen.

Greetings from Canada

In the Prairie
Dear Laar and Louis:

My best wishes and congratulations on Louis' birthday. I hope you'll have a good time and have many happy returns of this day. I am sorry I had no time to write.

I'll do so after a while. Betsy will tell you about my trip to here as soon as I have written her.

Yours, Jan Coops

You will get this card too late on account of the distance 40 miles from here to a town.

If not delivered return to Jan Coops, Meota, Sask. Canada

Coops farmed at NE 1/4 S-2, T-49, R-20 W of 2 Saskatchewan Homestead Index No: 1444502.

This card was mailed on April 2, 1907 by Jan Coops from North Battleford, Saskatchewan to Mrs. S. Bremer in Bussum. The Coops family also lived on the same street, at number 5, so Mrs. Bremer was likely once their neighbour.

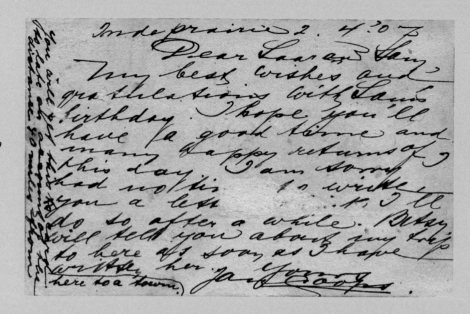

Dear Gina,

Many congratulations on your day, of December 5. We hope that you may celebrate that day enjoyably and in health many more times. Gina will write you soon again, where you now are. It was nice to receive a letter from you. It is winter here again. Twice there has been a mountain of snow. Greetings also for Jans. Soon, I will also write to her.

Now Gina, many greetings from your affectionate friend, G. Vos.

This card was mailed by G. Vos on November 22, 1914 from Calgary, Alberta to Gina van Doorn, c/o Miss A. Bos in The Hague. Annechien Bos was a servant for the dentist A. Uytenbogaart.

Dear Friend Alberts,

This serves in order to congratulate you on your birthday May you be granted many years still and celebrate with the other house members! That day brings me many memories. I always see Mother's last birthday! How she sat at the table, and yet gone so fast! That will occur also in your circle, there the death also has taken a sacrifice at yours. However that is the road of all flesh! Herewith, we wish you all a good New Year. May the New Year bring many blessings for you. With many greetings from Jans, Nico and Reijer.

Your affectionate friend, Mien [Wilhelmina]

Wilhelmina Aalten (b. May 29, 1888 in Zeist) married Nicolaas Donselaar (b. October 14, 1877 in Amersfoort) on May 29, 1913 in Nakusp.

This card was by Wilhelmina Donselaar-Aalten on December 15, 1913 from Nakusp, British Columbia to Gerrit Jan Alberts, a pastry baker in Zeist. Alberts was born December 22, 1857 in Leersum and died October 13, 1926 in Zeist.

S.S. Bonnington at Halcyon Hot Springs, Arrow Lakes, B.C.

Dear Treesje,

Many thanks for all the good wishes on my birthday.

Jo

A letter will follow . . .

This card was mailed on May 13, 1912 from Calgary, Alberta to Nijmegen and forwarded to Miss Ph. Bijvoet in Tilburg.

This card was mailed on January 27, 1908 from Toronto, Ontario to Arthur August Dullé in Amsterdam. Dullé was born March 11, 1878 in Ghent, Belgium. He was a travelling salesman.

Dear Friend,

Congratulations on Dina's birthday. Celebrate it freely and joyfully and I will, also.

Hearty handshake
from your friend, Han

10

Treasures From Home

This card was mailed by Jacques Smelt from Montreal, Quebec on November 19, 1910 to his brother, Johannes Th. M. Smelt in Weert, where he worked as an inspector for the Department of Public Works.

Dear Jan:

"If you get it, then you've got it." But I am not sure if they will mail this card. A while ago, I sent a picture postcard to Mother, but it came back because on such a card sent outside of Canada, one is not allowed to write on it. Pre-stamped cards [like this one] with a space for an answer, aren't available for foreign countries. Everything is fine. Yesterday I received Mother's letter.

Au revoir, comme on dit ici—
T. A. T. [tout à toi, all to you] Jacques

This card was mailed from Montreal, Quebec on February 16, 1912, to Miss R. Boltjes c/o Dr. Hoffman in Gouda. Dr. Albertus Cornelis Antonius Hoffman, was a well-known local medical doctor. He was born on March 4, 1868 in Leeuwarden and passed away in 1911 in Gouda.

A Winter Scene in Park Lafontaine, Montreal

Dear Miss,

Yesterday evening, when I came home from work, I found your letter. Let me thank you very much for that. Mother had just written to you the previous day and the letter was just put in a mail box. We all thought that you were angry or ill. You had written that it was also cold in Holland. Now, we also have our share. If you look at this card, you will recognize a well-known place.

Now, many greetings,
Betsy.

Letter will follow soon.

This card was mailed by Willem van Oeveren on September 8, 1911 from Chesley, Ontario to Hermanus Tweehuijsen in Haarlem. Hermanus was born July 27, 1881 in Haarlem, and became an engineer.

HARBOR, OWEN SOUND, CANADA.

Willem van Oeveren was born April 21, 1881 in Haarlem. He was re-moved from the Haarlem Municipal Record on August 21, 1906. According to the 1911 Census of Canada, he lived with his wife, Antje Hanenburg, together with her family, in Chesley, Ontario. Her father was Arjen Hanenburg, a butcher by trade. Her mother was Grietje Zevenberg who arrived in Canada in 1907.

Dear Friends:

Just a moment ago, we received your parcel with newspapers, and last week, your letter. My very many thanks for that. Pretty soon, I will write you a letter again. We are doing reasonably well. Today, it is exactly three years ago that we were married. And now your son is 3 years old, hearty felicitations.

Many greetings from both of us.

Mr. and Mrs. W. van Oeveren

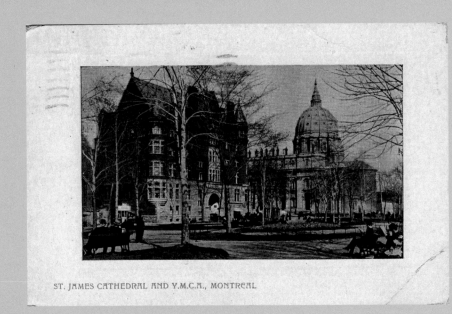

ST. JAMES CATHEDRAL AND Y.M.C.A., MONTREAL

This card was sent from Montreal, Quebec to Miss Jo Rutjes in Nijmegen on September 20, 1911, by Mauris F.C. van Geel.

Dear Madame:

Today, your picture postcards found me in good health, and I hope that you are also the same. So also, my thanks for your card which I found to be very pretty. Last week, I received a letter from Leonard and he is doing very well. Furthermore, I have no news, other than many greetings for all the acquaintances and the old gang, so also I wish you a pleasant time at the fair grounds.

From your future brother-in-law, M.F.C. v. Geel
Salu

Mauris was born February 14, 1884 in Wageningen.

Greetings from Canada

This card was mailed from Enderby, British Columbia on February 14, 1905, by Johan Goossen to his sister Frouke Abigael in Wons, Friesland. She was born on May 19, 1875 in Sint Annaland and married Arend Offringa on May 9, 1913 in Wonseradeel, Friesland.

Cara mia,

Letter received, therefore thanks, also Reins.

Write soon,

J. Goossen

Johan Goossen and his brother Pieter came to Canada in 1887 and settled first in Pilot Mound, Manitoba and then settled in the Enderby area of British Columbia. There they farmed the SE 1/4, S-28, T-18, R-7 W of 6th; the NE 1/4 S-24, T-18, R-8 W of 6th; and the NW 1/4 S-19, T-18, R-7, W of 6th. Johan Goossen was born May 24, 1864 and Pieter Goossen was born November 25, 1866, both in Vlissingen.

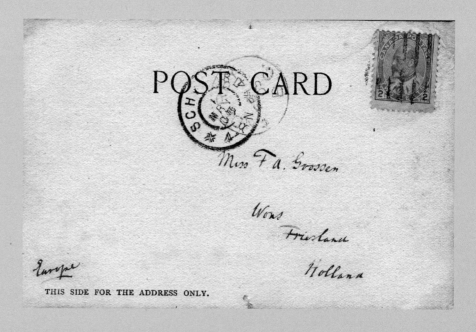

This card was mailed on August 18, 1908 from Chesley, Ontario to Froukje Nieland in Groningen. Her father, W. Nieland, was a painter.

A Residential Corner, Chesley.

Willem and Dorus are big boys now?

Dear Froukje,
Hereby, I am mailing you a picture postcard. I appreciated it very much that you mailed a card to me. I wish that more girls would do that. I do not know not all their addresses but perhaps they also do not know mine. It makes me think back again to the time—do you still remember when we went to school and played together. I think about that with pleasure. I get along here, but it is still not Holland (you know) because I have not as many friends as in Holland but I am, however, still happy. Greetings to aunt . . . and to your parents.

Many greetings from your old friend
Ienkje Hanenburg

Ienkje Hanenburg was born on September 29, 1892 in Groningen and emigrated to Canada in 1907 with her father, mother, and siblings. Her father was Arjen Hanenburg, born May 3, 1862 in Oudwoude.

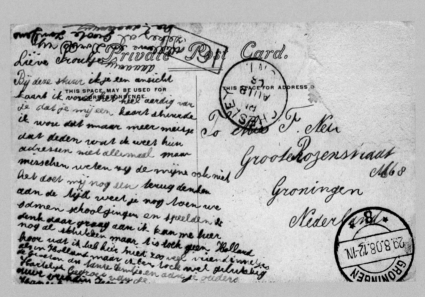

UNION BANK, WINNIPEG.

Dear Father and Mother,

I am still in good health and I hope for you both, the same. It is here already full winter. This is a bank building and I have been already at the top windows in order to drink some water. It is very easy here. All you need to do is walk into the elevator and in a second you are on the top. There are no water pumps on the road here.

Your son,

F. Scheffer

This card was sent on December 9, 1907 by Fransiscus Scheffer from Winnipeg, Manitoba to Johannes Bon in Naarden. Bon, a labourer, was born on October 3, 1841, and was married to Hermina Jansen, born February 8, 1836 in Klazinaveen.

This card was mailed on July 28, 1911 by E. Willems on July 28, 1911 from Toronto, Ontario to Rotterdam.

Dear Sirs!

Please provide an estimate to me by return mail for the cost of a one-year subscription for your Rotterdamse Nieuwsblad (& Sunday issue), to mail every week all papers from the week. And also let me know how you would like to be paid.

Yours faithfully,

E Willems (old Rotterdammer)
197 Bolton Avenue
Toronto, Canada.

The 1912 Toronto City directory shows Frank van der Ven de Visser as a shipper on 197 Bolton Ave.

This card was mailed by de Bakker on January 9, 1908 from Lamont, Alberta to Bodegraven.

Bird's Eye View of Edmonton, Alta.

Dear Sister:

I received your card this morning and I am very thankful for it.

Best wishes from your brother,

J. de Bakker

Jan Franciscus de Bakker, born in 1888, came to Canada in 1906 and worked as a carpenter.

This card was mailed on July 14, 1911 from Strathmore, Alberta to Miss Cristin van Poorte in Roozendaal.

AGRICULTURAL SCHOOL, STRATHMORE, ALTA. 1911.

Jos and Cor

Many greetings from both of us

Dear Miss and Cristin,

Today I received your letter with which we were very happy. To us it does not look good for Father. We have written him a letter and another note so that he can now go to the notary and they will read it for him and give him ten guilders.

I will write a letter to you, later.

Cor

This card was mailed on April 18, 1896 from Parry Sound, Ontario to Jacoba Constantia Loke in The Hague, (b. March 13, 1838 in Breda)

Dear Fl . . . je

I received the draft in order. Thanks for your effort. Until now, I have not succeeded with getting something— everywhere everything already occupied by older fellows. Perhaps I will go to help with reconstructing the burned down sawmill at McNeill in Orrville. Spring has arrived precipitately and it is very warm every day. All are well. Netie will write again one of these days. Jack has also recovered and is now busy exchanging his winter outfit for a summer outfit; he thanks you for your interest.

Our hearty greetings for you all.

Chris.

This card was mailed on February 9, 1911 from Fort William, Ontario to J. Opbroek in Haarlem.

Post Office, Fort William, Ont.

This is the Post Office.

Dear Annie

How are you? We are all right—your father and mother, also? I received your card! You know, Annie, if you would be here then you could go sleigh riding. I also still go to school and have learned quite a bit of English already. My mother does not understand me. Dirk is also doing very well at school. This afternoon I came back from being at that same school, and I played a spelling game with Father.

Now dear Annie, also greet your father and mother for me.

Your friend, Dirk [?]

Heinrich 'Harry' Steven Gerhard Nicolaas Horst was born in The Hague on January 12, 1874. He was married on October 20, 1896 in Utrecht to Johanna Wilhelmina Overdijking who was born on May 3, 1872 in Utrecht. According to the *Hilversumsche Courant*, in 1900 Horst ran a fish business in Hilversum called "De Gooische Vischhandel". He, his wife, son (probably Henry J.) and daughter (Hendrika Johanna Elisabeth, born August 9, 1905 in Hilversum) arrived in Quebec harbour on October 24, 1908 aboard the *Tunisian*. Horst farmed the SE 1/4 and SW 1/4 of S-30, T-21, R-19, W of 3rd in Saskatchewan. According to the 1911 Census, he owned a $2,000.00 life insurance policy, had crop insurance, and employed a few workers. (His wife does not appear in that census.)

This card was mailed on August 5, 1914 from Cabri, Saskatchewan to Martha Elisabeth Horst, Harry Horst's sister, in The Hague. Martha was born August 7, 1872 in The Hague. According to the municipal records, she took in boarders at the address on the card.

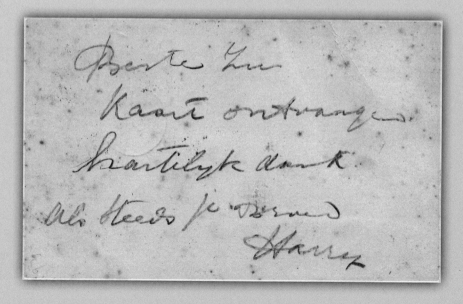

Dear Sister,

Received card. Many thanks. As always,

Harry

This card was mailed on August 12, 1907 from Nutana, Saskatchewan to Oss and then forwarded to Jo Koster in Hattem. Jo Koster (1868–1944) was a well-known painter in the Netherlands.

B.M.

I think that your postal parcel specifications must be incorrect. In Dutch money, a postal parcel from here is f 0.30 per English pound, that is 4½ hectograms or as you called it "an ounce". Thus a parcel, that weighs 9 ounces costs us f 0.60, 13½ ounce, f 0.90. The heaviest parcel weighs 11 pound thus 49½ ounces. That is almost 5 kilos and this costs f 3.30. Our address is not "Saskakchewan". Saskatchewan is the state or province, but the town called Nutana is one city with Saskatoon, thus Nutana is the right address. No need for more; it could have been the reason that we did not receive your letters.

With many greetings P. van B.

The sender is possibly Pieter van Bosse, the chief agent for the Netherlands-Canadian Mortgage Company (Ned-Canadeesche Hypotheekbank, Groningen).

From: L.F.H.
P.O. Box 1467
Edmonton, Alta
Canada

Edmonton, 1 Sep. 1909

Dear Uncle and Aunt,

I have heard from home that Justientje again has stayed for a while with you. I have to thank you that you have been so kind to her. Here, I often pass a wall with white flowers, morning glory, I believe they are called. Do you remember how I always made it difficult for you during the holiday times, and now, my daughter? It is very kind of you. Jacob will find this card very interesting. This is how railway tracks are laid with machines.

Many greetings to all of you from your nephew,

Bertus.

It appears that Lambertus Frederik Heuperman, age 26 and a widower, arrived in New York during February of 1908 aboard the *Rijndam*. While in Edmonton, he worked for Driscoll and Knight as a surveyor. During 1909, he and his brother (with the initials F.J.) moved to Calgary to work with another firm as surveyors on subdivisions in and around Calgary. Their reputations in this field were notable. It is not clear when he left Calgary, but his Attestation papers show that he joined the Canadian over-seas Expeditionary Force in 1918, when he was living in Hood River, Oregon, eventually serving in Siberia. Lambertus was married to Justina Frederika Verhoeve, sister-in-law of his uncle, Jacob Amesz, although the next of kin listed on the Attestation papers is Mrs. Violet Ethel Hazel Heuperman. He passed away in Salem, Oregon in 1962.

Lambertus F. Heuperman mailed this card from Edmonton, Alberta on September 1, 1909 to his uncle, Jacob Amesz, in Utrecht. Amesz was a typesetter, born in Gouda, March 19, 1856, and was married to Neeltje Verhoeve, who was born on February 10, 1858 in Amsterdam.

Longing to Hear from Home

INTERIOR OF A SALMON CANNERY SHOWING 60 000 CANS OF SALMON, NEW WESTMINSTER

This card was mailed by W.W. Van Dam on November 20, 1909 from Ft. MacLeod, Alberta to W.H. Verduijn at the Instituut Walburg in Arnhem. The institute provided schooling for military schools, technical schools, final exams, five-year high school (HBS), and admission exams for the Royal Dutch Academy (KMA). The director at this time was Mrs. Geuze.

Dear Brother,

Why don't you write me? You must write me pretty soon, a letter.

My address is W. W. Van Dam,
c/o Mr. Emmelkamp, Macleod,
Alberta, Canada.

Harm Emmelkamp, the owner of the farm that Van Dam was working at, was born October 20, 1867 in Jukwerd. He married Jantje Roos on March 15, 1890 in Grand Rapids, Michigan. He died in Calgary October 1, 1940. Jantje passed away on October 7, 1929 at Fort Macleod. Emmelkamp farmed the NE 1/4, S-28. T-10, R-25, W of 4th.

This card was mailed by Rietje [?] de Moor, on May 7, 1912 from Daysland, Alberta to P.G. de Moor in Zaamslag.

Dear Brother and Sister,

It has been a long time since I have heard something from you. I hope that you are both doing OK. When I get a letter, I shall write back, right away. We three of us are doing fine. Pretty soon I will send a small portrait of our little one. Many kisses from Elzye.

And many greetings,

Your loving sister, Rietje [?]

This card was mailed from Calgary, Alberta on October 5, 1910 to Miss Willy van der Lubben in The Hague. The address there is probably the business address of her father, a contractor and lumber dealer. The building at Number 18 Dunnebierkade was known as 'Zwitsershuis', which functioned as a lumber yard until 1946.

Dear Will,

Still nothing received. Haven't you been able to read the address correctly? I really believe that the letter has been lost. Did you receive my letters? Here is a picture of Sherbrooke. I am 2,000 km. farther, so that means, at the moment, I am 4,000 miles away from you.

631, 5 Avenue West, Calgary, Alberta.

King Street, looking towards Sherbrooke East, Sherbrooke, P.Q.

This card was mailed by Toon Vierveijzer, from Calgary, Alberta to Amsterdam on May 26, 1910.

Dear Mom:

Since March, I haven't received nor seen neither a card nor a brief from any of the others. What is going on? I am waiting longingly,
Toon

Anthonius Lambertus Cornelis Vierveijzer was born June 9, 1879 in Amsterdam. His parents were Antonie Johannes Vierveijzer and Anna Carolina Polman, both of Amsterdam.

This card was probably mailed from Montreal, Quebec (no cancel) to Johannes Vossen and was received on June 24, 1910 in Tilburg.

Dear Johann,

Are you guys still alive? I hear so little from you. The letter for you which I mailed rather late has not yet arrived. Write me soon.

Greetings,

Herman

Crescent Road, near South Drive, Rosedale, Toronto, Canada.

This card was mailed on May 19, 1915 from Toronto, Ontario to Marie Wiltschut in Overveen. Marie was probably a servant for the widow J.J. Enschedé. This family is well-known, leaving a historic name in the area around the city of Haarlem.

Dear Marie,

I meant to write you first a letter, but I had to write so much. I give you the new address of my sister and expect first, a letter from you. I am doing very well, I hope the same for you and Rijna, with greetings for her, also.

Address is 1 Muriel Ave. Toronto, Canada.

Geertje

Henri de Laat, age 23, came to Canada in 1906. According to the 1911 Census, he was working as a machine operator at the Knitting Factory, Woodstock, Ontario.

Dear Mr. Veenenbos,

Finally I am making myself known. You probably thought that I had forgotten you, but No, that is not the case, however, there is so little time to write. In one word, I can tell you that I am doing fine here. There couldn't be a better place to be. I have to work hard and it is also surprisingly hot here. I think than that one should earn his money by the sweat of one's face! And that is just the thing, because with such a temperature as it is here (the like of which one does not know in Holland) the drops drip along my face like the Niagara Falls. But anyway I am luckily very healthy and very satisfied. I hope to hear something from you, soon.

With hearty handshake from your friend, Henri de Laat

This card was mailed by Henri de Laat, July 6, 1908, from Princeton, Ontario to J. Veenenbos, Rotterdam. Veenenbos was the manager of the gin factory fa Tissot & Co. in Rotterdam, located on the Binnenweg. Also on the Binnenweg at that time was the Colonial merchandise business of W. J. de Laat. This is most likely their connection.

This card was mailed on April 19, 1911 from Toronto, Ontario to Zeist.

Dear Brother and Sister,

As you wrote, you had expected a letter from me. I am constantly planning to write, but every time it gets postponed. But now we shall, in a few days, we will cobble a letter together. We will send you also a photo of the house. I have a beautiful large photo camera.

Many greetings,
Your brother and sister, Kisses for Ma

Lefroy, [Ontario] March 12, 1914

Dear Geertje, Corrie and Beb;
How are you all? I don't hear anything. It is again 2 months ago that I received your last letter. I am doing fine here. It is really cold here. It is raw spring weather. I hope to see the summer soon. How is the weather in Holland—just like here?

Many Greetings, and kisses for dear Beb.
Your Brother, Martinus

This card was mailed from Bell Ewart, Ontario on April 13, 1914 to "Hoek, Esq." in Amsterdam. The address belongs to Gerrit Cornelis Hoek, born February 5, 1885 in Amsterdam. He was an office clerk. His wife was Johanna Geertruide Wijnders, born December 16, 1883 in Velsen. The child mentioned in the card is Elisabeth Cornelia, born September 18, 1902 in Buiksloot.

Greetings from Canada

This card was sent by Wilhelmina Schaufele from Alberta to Johanna (Jo) Meerholz and was stamped July 16, 1912 in Winterswijk. Jo's father, Albert Meerholz was an evangelist at the Vereninging van Vrienden der Waarheid, Nederlandse Hervormde Evangelisatie, in Winterswijk. He was born in 1866 in Amsterdam and passed away on March 6, 1944 in Hoogkerk.

Dear Jo!

Already it has been a long time since I have heard anything from you. Perhaps you didn't receive my last letter? At the moment we are all very healthy and I also hope to hear that from all of you. Are you still going to school and Dina still at the Normal School? It is also very warm here and also a lot of thunder and lightning. Greetings to all the girls at school and write back soon.

Greetings from Wilhelmina Schaufele

C.P.R. Passenger Train, Canadian Rockies

This card was mailed on April 29, 1913 from Nakusp, British Columbia to Miss H.S. van Lunteren in Zeist.

Dear S,

How come I don't hear anything from you? You must have received my letter and card, or are you perhaps ill??? I live worrying! Please s.v.p. let me hear something from you. How is your mother doing? You both receive my many greetings.

Your dearest, Mien
I am doing very well.

This card was mailed by Herman Pouwels to his father Pieter Pouwels Jr. in Bussum, from Winnipeg, Manitoba on July 5, 1912. His father, born December 31, 1851, in Amsterdam was a stockbroker. His mother was Hendrika Ernestina Elisabeth Blase, born April 12, 1856 in Amsterdam.

Have Henk and Marie received my letter? Winnipeg 5 July, 1912

Dear Parents,

It is now a month ago that I received your last letter dated May 24 and since then I have not received a sign of life from you. To be sure, I have been again and again to the post office, however I regularly return home empty-handed. Just because the messages about Father are far from rosy, I would appreciate that you answer my letters swiftly. Piet made the remark that I was so sparing with writing. It seems to me I proved the opposite because, since my stay here in Winnipeg, I have written you five times, of which four were letters, that is, on average, once a week. I look forward to receiving a message from you, soon. I am healthy, except for a slight cold. With my business, things go well. The next week I hope to write you a letter again, but I don't have time at the moment. To both of you, my warm-hearted greetings, and in thought a firm handshake from your loving son,

Herman.
My best wishes for Father.

Herman Pouwels was born April 17, 1885 in Amsterdam. ("Henk and Marie", referred to in his note, were Herman's brother Hendrik and sister Maria.)

12

Making Choices

Greetings from Canada

B.M., Sunnier than the summer home amidst the 1000 islands were the photographies of the sunniest kimono-dressed girls I ever saw on earth and which I could admire owing to Uncle John's obliging kindness. In the monotonous dreary and spirit-killing winter life of Berthier these fine pictures were like the mild beams of the glorious summer-sun. I need scarcely say which of the three sundry photos had my preference and which will always speak to me about a happy sweet time in your life, as I am sure.

I am about to come home at such date as will enable me to pass easier in the old country, where I wish to see you soon.

Yours devotedly, Gerard M.

Gerard J. M. Melchers, came to Canada in 1908 aboard the *Rijndam*. He was a member of the Melchers Distillers' family of Schiedam and Berthierville, Quebec. He would later marry Miss ten Bos. She belonged to a wealthy family who owned a well known spinning and weaving factory in Almelo.

This card was mailed on January 25, 1909 from Berthier-en-Haut, Quebec to Miss Wilhelmina J. M. ten Bos, in Almelo.

Dear Brother!

Likely you have already heard from mother, I will come again to Holland and if you still have shares, I would first like to find out what kind of factory it is, since the information I received diverged widely. Perhaps you cursed, but when I was working I did not feel like writing and that made mother concerned and she thought that I was ill; and then she phoned cousin Melchers to ask if he had received news from us. Now, I hope that before I am back you issued shares. Now, greetings to Anna, Jetje and many greetings from your loving brother, Jan.

Many congratulations, live long and in happiness with mom and child, and also congratulate . . . and Jetje.

This card was mailed on March 25, 1899 from Berthier en Haute, Quebec to Mr. W.A. van der Drift in Lochem.

Park Keeper's Residence, Mount Royal, Montreal

This card was mailed by Mauris van Geel on November 3, 1912 from Montreal, Quebec to his parents in Nijmegen. His father, Johan van Geel, was a policeman.

Dear Parents, Brothers, Sisters and children,

In the hope that you are all still very healthy, which for me is the case. I can also tell you that I will depart from here on the 13th, but I will write to you in any case when I expect to be in Holland. Concerning the weather here it is freezing again and furthermore is everything the same as before. Receive my further greetings for everyone,

from your son, M. van Geel

Well, goodbye and speedy reunion. Salu, see you.

Mauris would return to Canada.

This card was mailed by Mauris van Geel to his brother Leo, on April 13, 1913 from Montreal, Quebec to Bangsal-Modjokerto, Java, Dutch East Indies, after he had made his visit to the Netherlands in November of 1912.

My Dear Brother Leo,

In the hope that you are still healthy, which is also the case with me. Well Leonard, my compliments to you about that lovely service which you sent to Father and Mother; it is magnificent. Well Leo, most recently I have been in Holland for four months, but I did not have much pleasure. The reason is that it is very deathly and silent. There is no amusement, a cinema is all and here that is better and much cheaper. Well the summer starts here. At least today it is beautiful weather.

*Now, many greetings from your brother M v Geel
well, goodbye.*

173

This card was written from a train in the Ottawa area on October 17, 1913 to Anne Habermehl of Haarlem. Her father, J.H.W. Habermehl, was a teacher there.

Dear Anne,

On my way to Holland. Sunday I am in Montreal; Monday morning, New York; Tuesday I leave Hoboken on the S.S. Rotterdam. Hope to see and speak with you soon,

Many greetings
Yours, Phine

This card was mailed on May 31, 1912 from Toronto, Ontario to Klaas Flore, a wallpaper hanger, in Zeist.

Dear Brother and Sister.

Today our baggage has been expedited, thus we are coming. Sunday evening at 5:30 pm we are leaving from here and when you receive this card, we will already be close to you.

So D.Z., see you,
Greetings with kisses.

Dear Wife and child.

I am in the neighbourhood of Montreal, only one day, on November 28. I leave from Montreal with the steamship Lake Manitoba.

See you again, a thousand kisses from your man,

Toon

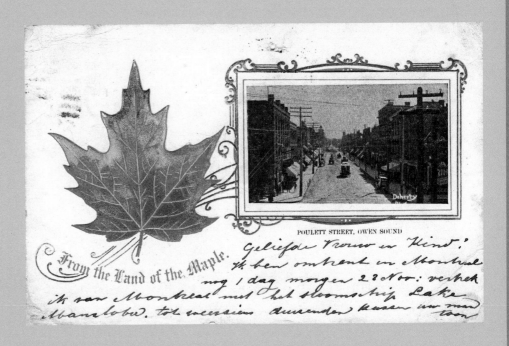

This card was mailed by Anthonius Cornelis Wouters (a beer bottler) on November 22, 1905 from Owen Sound, Ontario to Haarlem. He married Dieuwertje Geel on May 25, 1899 in Amsterdam. The child mentioned on the card is Neeltje Petronella, born January 21, 1903 in Amsterdam. This family would immigrate to Canada in March 1906, and resided in Winnipeg by 1907.

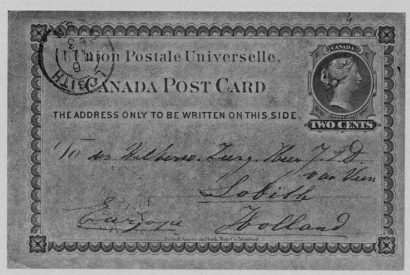

This card was mailed by Johan van Veen on April 21, 1893 from Chickney, Asiniboia to his father, The Reverend Johan Pieter Dionysius, in Lobith. Johan Sr. was born June 7, 1825 in Alkemade.

Dear Father and Sophia [his sister],

Coming Wednesday morning at 3 o'clock, I depart from Wolsely and on May 5 from New York with the "Teutonic" of the White Star Line. I depart so early from Wolsely because I have to be in Brandon for business and one day in Niagara. The train journey, without a stop takes 5 days, until the Toronto C.P.R.
Will write a card from Niagara and New York.

Now many greetings,
Johan.

Johan Pieter Dionysius was born November 7, 1866 in Krimpen a/d Lek and emigrated on April 14, 1892 to Canada. He had the means to visit his family in Holland and returned to his ranch near Chickney where he lived with his domestic aid, Edward Franks. The town of Chickney no longer exists but was located north of Lemberg and south of Abernethy, Saskatchewan.

Arrived here safely going to wpg tonight

3/8 1910

This card was mailed by Jan Lodewijk Waller on August 3, 1910 from Toronto, Ontario in Baarn, to his mother, Maria Frederika Waller. She was born January 19, 1850 in Amsterdam and passed away on May 4, 1932 in Utrecht.

He was his on his way back to his wife and children in Winnipeg after a trip to Netherlands. He arrived in New York from Antwerpen on the *Vaderland* of the Red Star Line. Being born into a family of wealthy Amsterdam financiers, he had the means to make a trip home to visit his family, unlike most immigrants.

Waller married Clara May Bull on September 21, 1904 in Winnipeg. He served for a short period as a Lieutenant in the Canadian army during the First World War. After five weeks at the front in France, he was admitted to hospital with synovitis and became unfit for battle. After the war, Waller pioneered for a number of years on a section of land (S-8, T-70, R-22, W of 5th) just north of the town of Valleyview in Northern Alberta. Waller passed away at aged 54 on March 9, 1934 in Edmonton. His wife, Clara, died September 12, 1977 in Sidney, British Columbia.

Dear Brother and Sister-in-law,

Hereby I am letting you know that I have received your picture postcards. And from those cards, I understand that you had already replied. Then perhaps your letter has been lost, which I feel bad about, but it will drift here and there in Canada. Furthermore, from Father and Marie, I found one at the post office here about six weeks after they were mailed. Those had been lying around somewhere, for sure. Other letters didn't arrive, at all. Furthermore, I can tell you that I won't write any letters anymore because I am planning to come home this winter, again. Then we can better talk about it. I am not badly off here, but most of them do in the beginning. But if I find out that it is still bad in Mokkem, then I will leave again with my wife, because without a wife it is not that easy, so long as you are OK with each other. Furthermore, many greetings from me,

Arie

From front of card:

This is a grain elevator and there are about six of them standing here. This is the life blood of Canada. The grain is loaded immediately into the boats.

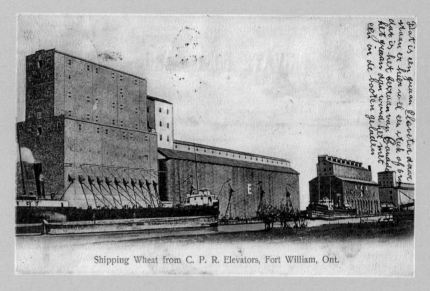

Shipping Wheat from C. P. R. Elevators, Fort William, Ont.

This card was mailed on August 8, 1904 by Arie van Leeuwen to G. van Leeuwen in Sloten.

'J.F. ten Hengel' is Johannes Frederik 'John' ten Hengel, born March 7, 1868 in Amsterdam, the son of Johannes Frederik ten Hengel and Margaretha Rijfkogel. His parents were married on April 4, 1867 in Amsterdam. In Rhenen, on May 18, 1898 John married Dirkje 'Dena' Kessel, born October 6, 1863 in Rhenen. In 1907, John left The Netherlands with his family. There were twin boys, Cornelis and Johan Frederik, born May 28, 1898 in Rhenen. It is not clear how long the family remained in Canada. According to the United States Federal Census for 1930, they were living in Morristown and Milburn, New Jersey.

This card was mailed to Willem van der Snoek, chief tram driver, on February 3, 1913, from Chesley, Ontario to Amsterdam. Willem was born on February 24, 1869 in Nieuwer-Amstel. His wife, Agatha Weinberg, was born on December 16, 1876 in Wormer. Their son, Reimer, was born on June 20, 1897 in Amsterdam.

CHESLEY FROM THE NORTH HILL.

Dear Mr. Van der Snoek,

Receive these cards in good health. I am doing very well and there is a good future for my boys. A letter will follow in 14 days.

I sent a card to your wife and two for Reinier.

Many greetings.
Yours, J.F. ten Hengel

179

Final Words

"Wij zeilen met verzegelde orders." 'We are sailing with sealed orders' is an old Dutch expression which means that the future is concealed from us; we do not know what life will bring us.

We could not foresee that a small collection of postcards would ever be compiled into a book, revealing messages from a handful of the millions of immigrants that have become part of the mosaic of Canada.

These Dutch immigrants sailed 'with sealed orders'. Dislocated from family and friends, filled with hope, they could not know how their lives would evolve in this new country. From the earliest days after arrival in Canada through to the time when they made the choice to stay, return or move on, they shared good news, bad news and life events that are common to us all. What remains interesting, and ever more moving, is the way that relating to the experience of another connects us. How many of us have waited for a reply to our letter, becoming more anxious the longer the delay? Or perhaps, experienced the lift in spirits upon receiving a note from one who is far away — a quick "hello" or short message that reaffirms their connection with us. The postcards were not intended to be seen by anyone other than those to whom they were written. However, we have taken the liberty of exposing them — revealing the honesty of these private messages, short, personal and often spontaneous, which directly touches our hearts with their intimacy.

It is practically inevitable that the snippets of information about both the senders and receivers of the postcards are incomplete. Moreover, there may well be errors, for which we take responsibility. Perhaps we have misread the writing, or simply missed a clue amongst the many along the trails that we followed in order to add more to the story. Genealogical work is detective work, and like all researchers, we also rely upon information from others, and are grateful for the contributions of those who shared more with us. With this in mind, we welcome corrections and additional information about these Dutch immigrants who, by sending a card to their old country, unintentionally contributed to our appreciation of the diverse immigration experience.

Endnotes

1. The term 'ego document' was probably first used by the historian Jacques Presser as a collective reference for autobiographies, memoirs, diaries, and personal letters. See: Arianne Baggerman and Rudolf Dekker, "De Gevaarlijkste Van Alle Bronnen, Egodocumenten: nieuwe wegen en perpectieven", *Tijdschrift voor Sociale en Economische Geschiedenis no.1* (2004).

2. Paul J. Vanderwood and Frank N. Samponaro, *Border Fury: A Picture Postcard Record of Mexico's Revolution and U.S. War Preparedness, 1910–1917* (Alberquerque, 1988), X.

3. Mary Lindeman, "Sources of Social History" in: *Encyclopedia of European Social History*, 6 vols. (Detroit: Charles Scribner's Sons, 2001), v. 1 p. 36.

4. David Prochaska and Jordanna Mendelson, Ed. *Postcards: Ephemeral Histories of Modernity* (University Park; The Pennsylvania State University Press, 2010, p. xi.

5. K.D. Bosch, *Nederlandse Beleggingen in de Verenigde Staten* (Amsterdam: Uitgeversmaatschappij Elsevier, 1958), p. 27.

6. *The Navigation Act* 1651.

7. Jan Th. J. Krijff, *Een Aengenaemen Vrientshap, An Amicable Friendship, A collection of historical events between the Netherlands and Canada from 1862 to 1914* (Toronto: Abbeyfield Publishers, 2003), p. 27.

8. Cees Zevenbergen, *Toen zij uit Rotterdam Vertrokken, Emigratie via Rotterdam door de Eeuwen Heen*, (Zwolle: Waanders Uitgevers, 1990), pp. 18–26.

9. Donald C. Mackay, Silversmiths and Related Craftsmen of the Atlantic Provinces (Halifax: Detheric Press, 1973), p. 63.

10. Jasper van der Sluys was baptized on September 15, 1784, in Geertruidenburg. On January 23, 1813 in Amsterdam, he married Maria Cornelia Roghe of Amsterdam. They attended St. Gabriel Presbyterian Church in Montreal. See also: John Halkett, *The Earl of Selkirk's Settlement: its Destruction and the Massacre of Governor Semple and his Party* (Bedford, Mass: Applewood Books, 2006), p. 166.

11. W.V. (Ben) Uttley, *A History of Kitchner* (Waterloo: Wilfrid Laurier University Press, 1975), p. 159.

12. *Het Nieuws van de Dag*, July 4, 1891.

13. Ileen Montijn, *Kermis Van Koophandel: De Amsterdamse Wereldtentoonstelling van 1883* (Bussum: Van Holkema & Warendorf, 1983).

14. J. Th. J. Krijff, *100 Years Ago, Dutch Immigration to Manitoba in 1893* (Windsor: Electa press, 1994) p. 17.

15. Klaas de Jong, *Cauliflower Crown*, Ed., Martha Knapp (Saskatoon: Western Producer Book Service, 1973) and John Harris, *The North*

American Dream, The Jake And Daisy Harris Family (Winnipeg, 1993).

16. *Algemeen Handelsblad*, July 15, 1897.
17. Rev. S. A. Schilstra was born August 31, 1840 in IJlst. He married Maria de Graaf in 1869 and emigrated to the USA in 1892. He died in 1916 in Telford, USA. He promoted Western Canada by writing articles in Dutch newspapers between 1902–1905.
18. *'t Vliegend Blaadje*, December 2, 1905.
19. *Nieuwsblad van Friesland*, March 23, 1912, Heerenveen.
20. *Advertentie Blad*, March 11, 1910.
21. *Hilversemsche Courant*, February 26, 1907.
22. Herman Ganzevoort, *A Bittersweet Land, The Dutch Experience in Canada*, 1890–1980 (Toronto: McClelland and Stewart, 1988). p. 27.
23. *Nieuwe Tilburgsche Courant*, November 19, 1908.
24. *De Rijnbode*, February 16, 1908.
25. *Het Nieuws van den Dag*, May 25, 1908.
26. From author's collection.
27. Donald Sinnema, *The First Dutch Settlement In Alberta: Letters from the Pioneer Years 1903–1914* (Calgary: University of Calgary Press, 2005).
28. Herman Ganzevoort, *The Last Illusion, Letters from Dutch Immigrants in the "Land of opportunity", 1924–1930* (Calgary: University of Calgary Press, 1999). p. 13.

Bibliography

Newspapers

Advertentie Blad
Algemeen Handelsblad
Hilversemsche Courant
Nieuwe Tilburgsche Courant
Nieuwsblad van Friesland
Het Nieuws van den Dag
't Vliegend Blaadje

Literature

• Baggerman, Arianne and Rudolf Dekker. "De Gevaarlijkste Van alle bronnen, Egodocumenten: nieuwe wegen en perspectieven", *Tijdschrift voor Sociale en Economische Geschiedenis*, No.1, 2004.

• Bosch, K.D. *Nederlandsche Beleggingen in de Verenigde Staten*. Amsterdam: Uitgeversmaatschappij Elzevier, 1958.

• Ganzevoort, Herman. *A Bittersweet Land, The Dutch Experience in Canada, 1890–1980*. Toronto: McClelland and Stewart, 1988.

• Ganzevoort, Herman. *A Dutch Homesteader on the Prairies, Willem de Gelder*. Toronto: University of Toronto Press, 1973.

• Ganzevoort, Herman. *The Last Illusion, Letters from Dutch Immigrants in the "Land of Opportunity", 1924-1930*. Calgary: University of Calgary Press, 1999.

• Krijff, Jan. Th. J. *100 Years Ago, Dutch Immigration to Manitoba in 1893*. Windsor: Electa Press, 1993.

• Krijff, Jan. Th. J. *Een Aengenaemen Vrientschap, An Amicable Friendship, A collection of historical events between the Netherlands and Canada from 1862 to 1914*. Toronto: Abbeyfield Publishers, 2003.

- Lindeman, Mary. "Sources of Social History" in: *Encyclopedia of European Social History,* Vol. 1 of 6 Vols. Detroit: Charles Scribner's Sons, 2001.

- Mackay, Donald. C. *Silversmiths and Related Craftsmen of the Atlantic Provinces.* Halifax: Detheric Press, 1973.

- Montijn, Ileen. *Kermis van Koophandel, de Amsterdamsche Wereldtentoonstelling van 1883.* Bussum: Van Holkema & Warendorf, 1983.

- Prochaska, David and Jordanna Mendelson, Eds. *Postcards: Ephemeral Histories of Modernity.* University Park: The Pennsylvania Sate University Press, 2010.

- Sinnema, Donald. *The First Dutch Settlement In Alberta: Letters from the Pioneer Years 1903–1914.* Calgary: University of Calgary Press, 1999.

- Uttley, W.V. (Ben). *A History of Kitchener.* Waterloo: Wilfrid Laurier University Press, 1975.

- Vanderwood, Paul, J and Frank N. Samponaro. *Border Fury: A Picture Postcard record of Mexico's Revolution and U.S. War Preparedness, 1910–1917.* Alberquerque: University of New Mexico, 1988.

- Zevenbergen, Cees. *Toen zij uit Rotterdam Vertrokken, Emigratie via Rotterdam door de Eeuwen Heen.* Zwolle: Waanders Uitgevers, 1990.

Referenced Online Sources for Genealogical Information

Canada

- http://www.ourroots.ca/search. aspx?qryID=DefaultBookBin_ID
- 1911 Census of Canada Indexing Project http:// automatedgenealogy.com/census11/
- Western Land Grants (Canada) http://www. collectionscanada.gc.ca/databases/western-land-grants/001007-100.01-e.php
- Nanaimo Family History Society http://members. shaw.ca/nanaimo.fhs/indexY.html
- Merrill Distad, (n.d.). "Postcard History". Retrieved from http://peel.library.ualberta.ca/postcardhistory. html
- http://www.ourontario.ca/demo/News.html
- http://www.torontofamilyhistory.org/toronto.html
- http://searches.rootsweb.ancestry.com/
- http://www.rootsweb.ancestry.com/~canns/ lunenburg/resources.html
- Soldiers of the First World War http://www. collectionscanada.gc.ca/databases/cef/001042-100.01-e.php
- http://search.bcarchives.gov.bc.ca/sn-1DFE1CD/ gbsearch/Deaths
- http://www.yorkton.ca/history/
- Obituary Index Peace River Record Gazette, 1932-1951 http://gp.abgensoc.ca/rg19321951.html
- http://www.archive.org/stream/n24sessionalpaper4 8canauoft/n24sessionalpaper48canauoft_djvu.txt

Netherlands

- Genlias Genealogy (Netherlands) http://www. genlias.nl/nl/search.jsp
- Central Bureau for Genealogy (Netherlands) http://194.171.109.12/page/459/ digitale%A0studiezaal
- 1915 Telephone Book (Netherlands) http://www. geneaknowhow.net/script/dewit/tel1915/
- http://www.stamboomzoeker.nl/
- http://kranten.kb.nl/
- http://www.stamboomforum.nl/
- http://frgen.andrysstienstra.nl/
- http://www.allegroningers.nl/
- http://www.allefriezen.nl/
- http://www.zeeuwengezocht.nl/en/
- http://www.hetutrechtsarchief.nl/collectie/ archiefbank/indexen/dtb
- http://haarlem.digitalestamboom.nl/
- http://stadsarchief.amsterdam.nl/archieven/ archiefbank/indexen/index.nl.html
- http://www.gemeentearchief.rotterdam.nl/ collectie/digitale-stamboom
- http://www.denhaag.nl/home/bewoners/to/ Stamboomonderzoek.htm
- http://www.groenehartarchieven.nl/
- http://www.geldersarchief.nl/familiegeschiedenis
- http://www.archiefleiden.nl/home/collecties/ personen/zoek-op-personen

- http://www.zaanstad.nl/bpo/publ_diensten/ gemeentearchief/genealogie/
- http://www.drenlias.nl/
- http://www.vlissingen.nl/Gemeentearchief/ Gemeentearchief/Genealogische-bronnen.htm
- http://zoeken.gooienvechthistorisch.nl/publiek/ detail.aspx?xmldescid=148558282
- http://www.streekarchiefvpr.nl/pages/nl/zoeken-in-collecties/genealogische-akten.php
- http://amersfoort.digitalestamboom.nl/%28oaa0lp 2vtz5z1hr2225ibv45%29/nl/home.asp
- http://www.vlaardingen.nl/stadsarchief/ Voorouders/id_10108968
- http://www.rhcrijnstreek.nl/index. php?option=com_content&task=category&section id=3&id=10&Itemid=24
- http://www.regionaalarchiefzutphen.nl/genealogie
- http://www.ecal.nu/familieonderzoek/
- http://www.regionaalarchieftilburg.nl/zoeken-in-databases/genealogie
- http://www.scribd.com/doc/76446972/7/ Generatie-7

Global

- http://newspaperarchive.com/northern-gazette/s

Index

Jan Krijff, B.A.(Economy), M.A. (History) was born in Delft, The Netherlands in 1947, also living in Nijmegen and Bloemendaal. After being schooled in Amsterdam as a pastry chef in 1968 he immigrated to Calgary, Alberta. While working at the Foothills Hospital, he attended Western High School. Afterwards, he attended the University of Calgary where he obtained a B.A. in Economics.

His second career started with the Canadian Imperial Bank of Commerce, which included a one-year posting in Resolute Bay, Nunavut (then the N.W.T.) He eventually returned home to The Netherlands, working for various airlines at Schiphol Airport, Amsterdam while he attended the University of Leiden. He graduated with a Master's degree in History in 1992.

Jan has combined his own experience with immigration, his connection with Canada and his fascination with history by exploring relations between the two countries, especially in the relatively unexplored period before World War I. In 1993, he published *100 Years Ago, Dutch immigration to Manitoba in 1893*. In 2003 he published *Een Aengenaeme Vrientschap, (An Amicable Friendship), A collection of historical events between The Netherlands and Canada from 1862 to 1914.*

Karen Green's family heritage includes the early settlement of southern Alberta, where so many immigrants, like her grandparents from Montana and Nebraska, chose to farm and raise their families. She was born in High River, Alberta, and grew up on the family farm near Brant. She attended County Central High School in Vulcan and received her degrees in Arts and Law at the University of Alberta in Edmonton.

Her law practice focused on employment and labour relations and human rights. It was this expertise that she brought to her work with local governments and community colleges, as well as teaching human resources management through the University of Victoria and Vancouver Community College. She has served as a member of the British Columbia Mental Health Review Board, working to ensure fair hearings for mental health patients. She also worked as a manager in learning and development with BC Hydro in Vancouver.

The important connecting thread for Karen through all of these experiences is the impact of people's stories, whether in the present, or as part of our collective history. She will now explore new horizons, as she herself becomes an immigrant, embarking on a move to Europe to learn new languages, among other things.